The Personal Promise Pocketbook

Harold Shaw Publishers
Wheaton, Illinois

Copyright © 1980
by Harold Shaw Publishers.
All rights reserved.
No part of this book
may be reproduced in any form
without written permission from
Harold Shaw Publishers, Box 567,
Wheaton, Illinois 60187.

Library of Congress Catalog Card Number 80-52398
ISBN 0-87788-673-3

First printing, July 1980
Second printing, September 1980
Third printing, October 1980
Fourth printing, March 1981
Fifth printing, June 1981
Sixth printing, July 1981
Seventh printing, October 1981

Printed in the United States of America

"This God—his way is
perfect; the promise of the
Lord proves true."
Psalm 18:30

Grateful acknowledgement is made to the publishers of the Scripture versions, portions of which are quoted in this book. After each verse the source of the reference is identified using the following abbreviations:

JB   THE JERUSALEM BIBLE
KJV   THE KING JAMES VERSION
NASB   THE NEW AMERICAN STANDARD BIBLE
NEB   THE NEW ENGLISH BIBLE
NIV   THE NEW INTERNATIONAL VERSION
NKJB   THE NEW KING JAMES BIBLE
Phillips   THE NEW TESTAMENT IN MODERN ENGLISH BY J. B. PHILLIPS
RSV   THE REVISED STANDARD VERSION
TEV   TODAY'S ENGLISH VERSION
TLB   THE LIVING BIBLE

Portions from:
THE JERUSALEM BIBLE Copyright 1966 © by Darton, Longman and Todd, Ltd., and Doubleday and Company, Inc. Used by permission of the publishers.
THE NEW AMERICAN STANDARD BIBLE, © the Lockman Foundation, 1960, 1962, 1963, 1965, 1971, 1972, 1973, 1975, and are used by permission.
THE NEW ENGLISH BIBLE, Copyright © the delegates of the Oxford University Press and the syndics of the Cambridge University Press, 1961, 1970. Reprinted by permission.
THE HOLY BIBLE, NEW INTERNATIONAL VERSION, Copyright © 1978 by New York International Bible Society. Used by permission.
THE NEW KING JAMES BIBLE, New Testament Copyright © 1979. Used by permission of Thomas Nelson, Publishers.
The Phillips' Translation reprinted with permission of the Macmillan Publishing Company, Inc., from the NEW TESTAMENT IN MODERN ENGLISH, revised edition by J. B. Phillips, © J. B. Phillips, 1958, 1960, 1972.
THE REVISED STANDARD VERSION OF THE BIBLE, Copyright 1946, 1952, © 1971, 1973.
The quotations from TODAY'S ENGLISH VERSION in this publication are from the GOOD NEWS BIBLE: Copyright © American Bible Society 1976. Used by permission.
THE LIVING BIBLE, Copyright 1971 by Tyndale House Publishers, Wheaton, Illinois. Used by permission.

How To Use Your Promise Book: The Four Way System

"This God—his way is perfect; the promise of the Lord proves true." (Psalm 18:30)

God's Word, the Bible, is full of promises—promises made to his children whom he loves. Because God is God, and his very nature is truth, he cannot be unfaithful to these promises. Everything that he has guaranteed to each of us, we can trust him to carry out completely.

As you use this PERSONAL PROMISE POCKET-BOOK, remember that these verses are God's guarantees to you, his child. Through prayer and practice, these promises can become part of your life, giving you hope, joy and victory.

Step One:
Ask yourself, "In what area of my life do I need to hear God's Word? What are my feelings right now? What are my struggles?" Turn to the Promise Index and find the section that *asks your question*, that fits your present situation. Read the verses slowly, carefully, letting his Word fill your heart and mind.

Step Two:
Choose one of the verses which speaks to you, that touches you and check the first box next to that promise. Then write today's date in the space provided. Claim this verse as God's guarantee to you today! Know that he has given it to you! (You may want to look it up in your Bible and read it in its context).

Step Three:

Copy the verse on a notecard so that you can keep it with you, and memorize it. Memorizing comes quickly and easily when you read the verse several times a day. Tape it to the dashboard of your car, your school notebook, your bathroom mirror, your desk or bulletin board—wherever you're sure to see it often and claim it as your own.

Step Four:

Turn to the prayer page at the end of the book or use the reverse side of your memory card and write a short prayer to God thanking Him for his promise to you (state it specifically in terms of your situation) and claim the promise for your own life.

Applying the Four Way System

Here are some illustrations of how the Promise Book may be used, whether you are a young person or an older person.

Another member of your school basketball team has made some nasty comments about your game skills. To make things worse, this person is the only other Christian on the team! God's promise to you in this situation might be one found on page 96 of this Promise Book:

Be humble and gentle. Be patient with each other, making allowance for each other's faults because of your love. Try always to be led along together by the Holy Spirit, and so be at peace with one another. *Ephesians 4:2, 3 (TLB)*.

Here's a prayer you could write: "Lord, I forgive Sandy for those cutting remarks. Make me more loving and co-operative. Help me to be a good team-mate and a better player. Join Sandy's spirit and mine in your love so that we can show others how well Christians get along. In Jesus' name. Amen."

Or, perhaps you have been anxious because of an urgent financial need, or bad health. In response to the promise on page 68:

Don't worry about anything, but in all your prayers ask God for what you need, always asking him with a thankful heart. And God's peace, which is far beyond human understanding, will keep your hearts and minds safe in union with Christ Jesus. *Philippians 4:5, 7 (TEV)*,

you may record a prayer like this: "Lord, I choose not to panic in this emergency. You know how much surgery costs and what my salary is. Because you love me, I believe you will not only supply the funds but calm my fears until this is all over. Thank you, Jesus, my Lord. Amen."

Or, you may feel that your spiritual life has dried up. You're miserable about your emptiness and lack of joy in God. This verse on page 75 may be the promise for you:

Whoever drinks of the water that I shall give him will never thirst; the water that I shall give him will become in him a spring of water welling up to eternal life. *John 4:14 (NIV)*.

If your heart responds to these words, your prayer may be: "Holy Spirit, I need the water of your life to quench my thirst. Satisfy me with yourself so that I can be a green and growing Christian. In Jesus' name. Amen."

Finally

As God's promise becomes reality and you recognize the fulfillment of his Word to you, check the second box and fill in the date. And remember, if God's promises are true now, they will prove true tomorrow and he will continue to carry them out again and again for the rest of your life!

Your Index To God's Promises

Section 1:
God's Promises and Purposes for Me

Section 2:
God's Promises and Purposes for My Relationship with Him

• I feel spiritually dry. Will God fill me with his abundant life? 74

• I want to worship God, but I'm not sure how. Will he show me how to worship him acceptably? 75

• God has given me so much. What response does he want from me? 77

Section 3:
God's Promises and Purposes for My Relationships with Others

• I am grateful that God has forgiven me. But how does this affect my relationships with others? 79

• I have trouble being kind to people who don't like me; who hurt me. How should I respond to the hostility of others? 80

• God is good to everyone. I want to be like him, but *how*? 81

• Other people's actions often irritate me. How much tolerance and patience does God expect of me? 83

• I know God wants me to be generous. If I give freely, how can I be sure I won't be left destitute myself? 85

• So often, other people have what I want. How can I deal with my jealousy? 86

• I really want to love other people. Will God show me how to love? 87

• My parents don't always understand me. How should I respond to them? 88

• I always seem to argue with my brothers and sisters. Will God help me to form better relationships with them? 90

God's Promises and Purposes for Me

_____

I'm unsure of my identity. Lord, who am I?

1. God created man in his own image, in the image of God he created him; male and female he created them. *Genesis 1:27 (RSV)*
□ _____ □ _____

2. You made him a little lower than the heavenly beings and crowned him with glory and honor. *Psalm 8:5 (NIV)* □ _____ □ _____

3. Through the living and eternal word of God you have been born again as the children of a parent who is immortal, not mortal. *I Peter 1:23 (TEV)*
□ _____ □ _____

4. Now that you have faith in Christ Jesus you are all sons of God. *Galatians 3:26 (Phillips)*
□ _____ □ _____

5. You are no longer foreigners and aliens, but fellow citizens with God's people and members of God's household. *Ephesians 2:19 (NIV)*
□ _____ □ _____

6. Through God you are no longer a slave but a son, and if a son then an heir. *Galatians 4:7 (RSV)*
□ _____ □ _____

7. I no longer call you slaves, for a master doesn't confide in his slaves; now you are my friends. *John 15:15 (TLB)* □ _____ □ _____

8. We who believe are carefully joined together with Christ as parts of a beautiful, constantly growing temple for God. And you also are joined with him and with each other by the Spirit, and are part of this dwelling place of God. *Ephesians 2:21, 22 (TLB)*
□ _____ □ _____

9. We Christians . . . can be mirrors that brightly reflect the glory of the Lord. And as the Spirit of the Lord works within us, we become more and more like him. *II Corinthians 3:18 (TLB)*

☐ _____ ☐ _____

I have decisions to make. Will God guide me and give me purpose?

1. If you want to know what God wants you to do, ask him, and he will gladly tell you, for he is always ready to give a bountiful supply of wisdom to all who ask him. *James 1:5 (TLB)*

☐ _____ ☐ _____

2. The Lord guides a man in the way he should go and protects those who please him. *Psalm 37:23 (TEV)* ☐ _____ ☐ _____

3. You chart the path ahead of me and tell me where to stop and rest. Every moment, you know where I am. You both precede and follow me, and place your hand of blessing on my head. *Psalm 139:3, 5 (TLB)*

☐ _____ ☐ _____

4. He guides the humble in what is right and teaches them his way. *Psalm 25:9 (NIV)*

☐ _____ ☐ _____

5. Just as you trusted Christ to save you, trust him, too, for each day's problems; live in vital union with him. *Colossians 2:6 (TLB)*

☐ _____ ☐ _____

6. Do not be anxious about tomorrow, for tomorrow will be anxious for itself. Let the day's own trouble be sufficient for the day. *Matthew 6:34 (RSV)*

☐ _____ ☐ _____

7. I will teach you what you are to do. *Exodus 4:15 (NASB)* ☐ _____ ☐ _____

8. We know that to those who love God, who are called according to his plan, everything that happens fits into a pattern for good. *Romans 8:28 (Phillips)*
☐ _____ ☐ _____

9. The Lord will fulfill his purpose for me; your love, O Lord, endures forever. *Psalm 138:8 (NIV)*
☐ _____ ☐ _____

10. I will instruct you (says the Lord) and guide you along the best pathway for your life; I will advise you and watch your progress. *Psalm 32:8 (TLB)*
☐ _____ ☐ _____

Life is very confusing. Will God help me to see clearly?

1. God is not a God of confusion but of peace. *I Corinthians 14:33 (RSV)*
☐ _____ ☐ _____

2. If any of you lacks wisdom, he should ask God, who gives generously to all without finding fault, and it will be given to him. *James 1:5 (NIV)*
☐ _____ ☐ _____

3. You, being rooted and grounded in love, may have power to comprehend with all the saints what is the breadth and length and heighth and depth, and to know the love of Christ which surpasses knowlegde, that you may be filled with all the fullness of God. *Ephesians 3:17-19 (RSV)*
☐ _____ ☐ _____

4. Where you have envy and selfish ambition, there you find disorder and every evil practice. But the wisdom that comes from heaven is first of all pure; then peace-loving, considerate, submissive, full of mercy and good fruit, impartial and sincere. *James 3:16, 17 (NIV)* ☐ _____ ☐ _____

5. He has made known to us in all wisdom and insight the mystery of his will, according to his purpose which he set forth in Christ. *Ephesians 1:9 (RSV)*

□ _____ □ _____

6. Behold, Thou dost desire truth in the innermost being, and in the hidden part Thou wilt make me know wisdom. *Psalm 51:6 (NASB)*

□ _____ □ _____

7. For the Lord gives wisdom, and from his mouth come knowledge and understanding. *Proverbs 2:6 (NIV)* □ _____ □ _____

8. Your Teacher will not hide himself any more, but your eyes shall see your Teacher. And your ears shall hear a word behind you, saying, "This is the way, walk in it," when you turn to the right or when you turn to the left. *Isaiah 30:20, 21 (RSV)*

□ _____ □ _____

I feel depressed, desperate. Where's the light at the end of the tunnel?

1. The Lord your God is with you; his power gives you victory. The Lord will take delight in you, and in his love he will give you new life. *Zephaniah 3:17 (TEV)*

□ _____ □ _____

2. I have come in order that you might have life, life in all its fullness. *John 10:10 (TEV)*

□ _____ □ _____

3. Base your happiness on your hope in Christ. When trials come endure them patiently; steadfastly maintain the habit of prayer. *Romans 12:12 (Phillips)*

□ _____ □ _____

4. If God is for us, who can be against us? *Romans 8:31 (NIV)* □ _____ □ _____

5. Only test me! Open your mouth wide and see if I won't fill it. You will receive every blessing you can use! *Psalm 81:10 (TLB)* □＿＿＿＿＿ □＿＿＿＿＿

6. We are able to hold our heads high no matter what happens and know that all is well, for we know how dearly God loves us, and we feel this warm love everywhere within us because God has given us the Holy Spirit to fill our hearts with his love. *Romans 5:5 (TLB)* □＿＿＿＿＿ □＿＿＿＿＿

7. Those who sow in tears will reap with songs of joy. *Psalm 126:5 (NIV)* □＿＿＿＿＿ □＿＿＿＿＿

8. Tears may flow in the night, but joy comes in the morning. *Psalm 30:5 (TEV)* □＿＿＿＿＿ □＿＿＿＿＿

9. My people shall be satisfied with my goodness, says the Lord. *Jeremiah 31:14 (RSV)* □＿＿＿＿＿ □＿＿＿＿＿

10. The Lord is close to the brokenhearted and saves those who are crushed in spirit. *Psalm 34:18 (NIV)* □＿＿＿＿＿ □＿＿＿＿＿

11. I waited patiently for the Lord; he turned to me and heard my cry. He lifted me out of the slimy pit; out of the mud and mire; he set my feet on a rock and gave me a firm place to stand. *Psalm 40:1, 2 (NIV)* □＿＿＿＿＿ □＿＿＿＿＿

12. Why am I so sad? Why am I so troubled? I will put my hope in God, and once again I will praise him, my savior and my God. *Psalm 42:11 (TEV)* □＿＿＿＿＿ □＿＿＿＿＿

13. Praise the Lord, O my soul; all my inmost being, praise his holy name. Praise the Lord, O my soul, and forget not all his benefits. He forgives all my sins and heals all my diseases; he redeems my life from the pit and crowns me with love and compassion. He satisfies my desires with good things, so that my youth is renewed like the eagle's. *Psalm 103:1-5 (NIV)* □＿＿＿＿＿ □＿＿＿＿＿

Everything has been going wrong lately. Will God help me in my daily work?

1. Commit to the Lord whatever you do, and your plans will succeed. *Proverbs 16:3 (NIV)*
☐ _____ ☐ _____

2. Take courage . . . work, for I am with you, says the Lord of hosts . . . my Spirit abides among you; fear not. *Haggai 2:4 (RSV)* ☐ _____ ☐ _____

3. Don't be discouraged, any of you. Do the work, for I am with you. *Haggai 2:4 (TLB)*
☐ _____ ☐ _____

4. Thus says the Lord, your Redeemer, the Holy One of Israel: "I am the Lord your God, who teaches you to profit, who leads you in the way you should go." *Isaiah 48:17 (NASB)* ☐ _____ ☐ _____

5. Commit everything you do to the Lord. Trust him to help you do it and he will. *Psalm 37:5 (TLB)*
☐ _____ ☐ _____

6. Blessed is the man who does not walk in the counsel of the wicked or stand in the way of sinners or sit in the seat of mockers. But his delight is in the law of the Lord, and on his law he meditates day and night. He is like a tree planted by streams of water, which yields its fruit in season and whose leaf does not wither. Whatever he does prospers. *Psalm 1:1-3 (NIV)*
☐ _____ ☐ _____

7. Wisdom and knowledge will be given you. And I will also give you wealth, riches and honor. *II Chronicles 1:12 (NIV)* ☐ _____ ☐ _____

8. I myself will go with you and give you success. *Exodus 33:14 (TLB)*
☐ _____ ☐ _____

I feel bound by bad attitudes and wrong habits. Will God release me from them?

1. If the Son sets you free, you will be free indeed. *John 8:36 (NIV)*

☐ _____ ☐ _____

2. If you hold to my teaching, you are really my disciples. Then you will know the truth, and the truth will set you free. *John 8:31 (NIV)*

☐ _____ ☐ _____

3. Wherever the Spirit of the Lord is, men's souls are set free. *II Corinthians 3:17 (Phillips)*

☐ _____ ☐ _____

4. I, the Lord your God, brought you out of Egypt so that you would no longer be slaves. I broke the power that held you down and let you walk with your head held high. *Leviticus 26:13 (TEV)*

☐ _____ ☐ _____

5. You have shattered the yoke that burdens them, the bar across their shoulders, the rod of their oppressor. *Isaiah 9:4 (NIV)*

☐ _____ ☐ _____

6. You who were once slaves of sin have become obedient from the heart . . . and having been set free from sin have become slaves of righteousness. *Romans 6:17, 18 (RSV)*

☐ _____ ☐ _____

7. We should no longer be slaves to sin—because anyone who has died has been freed from sin. *Romans 6:6, 7 (NIV)* ☐ _____ ☐ _____

8. For freedom Christ has set us free; stand fast therefore and do not submit again to a yoke of slavery. *Galatians 5:1 (RSV)*

☐ _____ ☐ _____

I feel so very much alone. Does God understand?

1. I am not going to leave you alone in the world—
I am coming to you. *John 14:18 (Phillips)*
□ _____ □ _____

2. He gives the lonely a home to live in and leads
prisoners out into happy freedom. *Psalm 68:6 (TEV)*
□ _____ □ _____

3. You will call, and the Lord will answer; you will cry,
and He will say, "Here I am." *Isaiah 58:9 (NASB)*
□ _____ □ _____

4. The nearer you go to God, the nearer he will come
to you. *James 4:8 (JB)*
□ _____ □ _____

5. The Lord your God is with you . . . He will take great
delight in you, he will quiet you with his love, he will
rejoice over you with singing. *Zephaniah 3:17 (NIV)*
□ _____ □ _____

6. Your Creator will be your husband. The Lord of
Hosts is his name. *Isaiah 54:5 (TLB)*
□ _____ □ _____

7. I will betroth you to me forever. *Hosea 2:19 (NIV)*
□ _____ □ _____

8. You have everything when you have Christ, and
you are filled with God through your union with Christ.
Colossians 2:10 (TLB)
□ _____ □ _____

9. The friendship of the Lord is for those who fear
him, and he makes known to them his covenant. *Psalm
25:14 (RSV)* □ _____ □ _____

10. Remember, I will be with you and protect you
wherever you go . . . I will not leave you until I have
done all that I have promised you. *Genesis 28:15
(TEV)* □ _____ □ _____

I'm afraid. Where can I turn for help?

1. Don't be afraid for the Lord will go before you and will be with you; he will not fail nor forsake you. *Deuteronomy 31:8 (TLB)*

☐ _____ ☐ _____

2. The Lord who created you says, "Do not be afraid—I will save you. I have called you by name— you are mine. When you pass through deep waters, I will be with you; your troubles will not overwhelm you." *Isaiah 43:1, 2 (TEV)*

☐ _____ ☐ _____

3. God is our shelter and strength, always ready to help in times of trouble. So we will not be afraid, even if the earth is shaken and mountains fall into the ocean depths. *Psalm 46:1, 2 (TEV)*

☐ _____ ☐ _____

4. He will never let me stumble, slip or fall. For he is always watching, never sleeping. Jehovah himself is caring for you! He is your defender. He protects you day and night. He keeps you from all evil, and preserves your life. He keeps his eye upon you as you come and go, and always guards you. *Psalm 121:3-8 (TLB)* ☐ _____ ☐ _____

5. The name of the Lord is a strong tower; the righteous run to it and are safe. *Proverbs 18:10 (NIV)*

☐ _____ ☐ _____

6. I am convinced that neither death nor life, neither angels nor demons, neither the present nor the future, nor any powers, neither height nor depth, nor any- thing else in all creation, will be able to separate us from the love of God that is in Christ Jesus our Lord. *Romans 8:38, 39 (NIV)*

☐ _____ ☐ _____

7. God has not given us a spirit of fear, but of power and of love and of a sound mind. *II Timothy 1:7 (NKJB)* ☐ _____ ☐ _____

8. His peace will keep your thoughts and your hearts quiet and at rest as you trust in Christ Jesus. *Philippians 4:7 (TLB)*

☐_____ ☐_____

I'm really in trouble. Will God rescue me?

1. Call upon Me in the day of trouble; I shall rescue you, and you will honor Me. *Psalm 50:15 (NASB)*

☐_____ ☐_____

2. In this world you will have trouble. But take heart! I have overcome the world. *John 16:33 (NIV)*

☐_____ ☐_____

3. Jehovah himself is caring for you! He is your defender. He protects you day and night. He keeps you from all evil, and preserves your life. He keeps his eye upon you as you come and go, and always guards you. *Psalm 121:5-8 (TLB)*

☐_____ ☐_____

4. He does not ignore the prayers of men in trouble when they call to him for help. *Psalm 9:12 (TLB)*

☐_____ ☐_____

5. The Lord saves righteous men and protects them in times of trouble. He helps them and rescues them. *Psalm 37:39, 40 (TEV)*

☐_____ ☐_____

6. The Angel of the Lord guards and rescues all who reverence him. *Psalm 34:7 (TLB)*

☐_____ ☐_____

7. God is our shelter and strength, always ready to help in times of trouble. *Psalm 46:1 (TEV)*

☐_____ ☐_____

8. When I am surrounded by troubles, you keep me safe. You oppose my angry enemies and save me by your power. *Psalm 138:7 (TEV)*

☐_____ ☐_____

Grief is overwhelming me. Will God reach down and comfort me?

1. Blessed be the God and Father of our Lord Jesus Christ, a gentle Father and the God of all consolation who comforts us in all our sorrows, so that we can offer others, in their sorrows, the consolation that we have received from God ourselves. *II Corinthians 1:3, 4 (JB)* □ _____ □ _____

2. May our Lord Jesus Christ himself and God our Father, who has loved us and given us everlasting comfort and hope which we don't deserve, comfort your hearts with all comfort, and help you in every good thing you say and do. *II Thessalonians 2:16, 17 (TLB)* □ _____ □ _____

3. My comfort in my suffering is this: Your promise renews my life. *Psalm 119:50 (NIV)*
□ _____ □ _____

4. Even though I walk through the valley of the shadow of death, I fear no evil; for Thou art with me; Thy rod and Thy staff, they comfort me. *Psalm 23:4 (NASB)* □ _____ □ _____

5. You will increase my honor and comfort me once again. *Psalm 71:21 (NIV)*
□ _____ □ _____

6. Comfort, Oh, comfort my people, says your God. Speak tenderly to Jerusalem and tell her that her sad days are gone. *Isaiah 40:1, 2 (TLB)*
□ _____ □ _____

7. The Lord will comfort Zion: he will comfort all her waste places, and will make her wilderness like Eden, her desert like the garden of the Lord; joy and gladness will be found in her, thanksgiving and the voice of song. *Isaiah 51:3 (RSV)*
□ _____ □ _____

8. He has sent me . . . to comfort all who mourn . . . to bestow on them . . . the oil of gladness instead of

mourning, and a garment of praise instead of a spirit of despair. *Isaiah 61:1-3 (NIV)*
☐ _____ ☐ _____

9. As a mother comforts her child, so will I comfort you. *Isaiah 66:13 (NIV)*
☐ _____ ☐ _____

10. I will turn their mourning into gladness; I will give them comfort and joy instead of sorrow. *Jeremiah 31:13 (NIV)* ☐ _____ ☐ _____

I'm too tired to cope. God, will you give me strength?

1. He gives power to the tired and worn out, and strength to the weak. *Isaiah 40:29 (TLB)*
☐ _____ ☐ _____

2. My grace is all you need; for my power is strongest when you are weak. *II Corinthians 12:9 (TEV)*
☐ _____ ☐ _____

3. Be strong—not in yourselves but in the Lord, in the power of his boundless strength. *Ephesians 6:10 (Phillips)* ☐ _____ ☐ _____

4. I have strength for anything through him who gives me power. *Philippians 4:13 (NEB)*
☐ _____ ☐ _____

5. His weak, human body died on the cross, but now he lives by the mighty power of God. We, too, are weak in our bodies, as he was, but now we live and are strong, as he is, and have all of God's power. *II Corinthians 13:4 (TLB)*
☐ _____ ☐ _____

6. The God of Israel gives power and strength to his people. *Psalm 68:35 (NIV)*
☐ _____ ☐ _____

7. Fear not, for I am with you, be not dismayed, for I

am your God; I will strengthen you, I will help you, I will uphold you with my victorious right hand. *Isaiah 41:10 (RSV)* ☐ _____ ☐ _____

8. Come to me, all you who are weary and burdened, and I will give you rest. *Matthew 11:28 (NIV)*
☐ _____ ☐ _____

9. As a father has compassion on his children, so the Lord has compassion on those who fear him; for he knows how we are formed, he remembers that we are dust. *Psalms 103:13, 14 (NIV)*
☐ _____ ☐ _____

10. Trust in the Lord God always, for in the Lord Jehovah is your everlasting strength. *Isaiah 26:4 (TLB)* ☐ _____ ☐ _____

I have problems with poor health. What can God do for me?

1. "I will restore you to health and I will heal you of your wounds," declares the Lord. *Jeremiah 30:17 (NASB)* ☐ _____ ☐ _____

2. I am the Lord, your healer. *Exodus 15:26 (RSV)*
☐ _____ ☐ _____

3. Prayer, made in faith, will heal the sick person; the Lord will restore him to health, and the sins he has committed will be forgiven. *James 5:15 (TEV)*
☐ _____ ☐ _____

4. He personally bore our sins in his own body on the cross, so that we might be dead to sin and be alive to all that is good. It was the suffering that he bore which has healed you. *I Peter 2:24 (Phillips)*
☐ _____ ☐ _____

5. Is anyone among you suffering? Let him pray. *James 5:13 (NKJB)*
☐ _____ ☐ _____

6. I will always guide you and satisfy you with good things. I will keep you strong and well. You will be like a garden that has plenty of water, like a spring of water that never runs dry. *Isaiah 58:11 (TEV)*
☐ _____ ☐ _____

7. (Jesus) healed all who were sick. This was to fulfil what was spoken by the prophet Isaiah, "He took our infirmities and bore our diseases." *Matthew 8:16, 17 (RSV)* ☐ _____ ☐ _____

8. Faith in Jesus' name—faith given us from God— has caused this perfect healing. *Acts 3:16 (TLB)*
☐ _____ ☐ _____

9. For you who fear my name the sun of righteousness shall rise, with healing in its wings. *Malachi 4:2 (RSV)* ☐ _____ ☐ _____

I worry about my appearance. How does God view me?

1. The Lord does not look at the things man looks at. Man looks at the outward appearance, but the Lord looks at the heart. *I Samuel 16:7 (NIV)*
☐ _____ ☐ _____

2. You should not use outward aids to make yourselves beautiful, such as the way you do your hair, or the jewelry you put on, or the dresses you wear. Instead your beauty should consist of your true inner self, the ageless beauty of a gentle and quiet spirit, which is of the greatest value in God's sight. *I Peter 3:3, 4 (TEV)* ☐ _____ ☐ _____

3. Charm is deceptive, and beauty is fleeting; but a woman who fears the Lord is to be praised. *Proverbs 31:30 (NIV)* ☐ _____ ☐ _____

4. Worship the Lord with the beauty of holy lives. *Psalms 96:9 (TLB)* ☐ _____ ☐ _____

5. He has made everything beautiful in its time. *Ecclesiastes 3:11 (RSV)*

☐ _____ ☐ _____

6. You will be a crown of beauty in the hand of the Lord, and a royal diadem in the hand of your God. *Isaiah 62:3 (NASB)*

☐ _____ ☐ _____

7. The Lord their God will save them on that day as the flock of his people. They will sparkle in his land like jewels in a crown. How attractive and beautiful they will be! *Zechariah 9:16, 17 (NIV)*

☐ _____ ☐ _____

I'm full of anxiety. God, where can I find peace?

1. I am leaving you with a gift—peace of mind and heart! And the peace I give isn't fragile like the peace the world gives. So don't be troubled or afraid. *John 14:27 (TLB)* ☐ _____ ☐ _____

2. I have told you all this so that you may find peace in me. In the world you will have trouble, but be brave: I have conquered the world. *John 16:33 (JB)*

☐ _____ ☐ _____

3. To be controlled by human nature results in death; to be controlled by the Spirit results in life and peace. *Romans 8:6 (TEV)* ☐ _____ ☐ _____

4. Do not be anxious about your life, what you shall eat, nor about your body, what you shall put on. For life is more than food and the body more than clothing . . . which of you by being anxious can add a cubit to his span of life? *Luke 12:22, 23, 25 (RSV)*

☐ _____ ☐ _____

5. You will keep in perfect peace him whose mind is

steadfast, because he trusts in you. *Isaiah 26:3 (NIV)*
□ _____ □ _____

6. In peace I will both lie down and sleep, for Thou alone, O Lord, dost make me to dwell in safety. *Psalm 4:8 (NASB)* □ _____ □ _____

7. The Lord gives strength to his people; the Lord blesses his people with peace. *Psalm 29:11 (NIV)*
□ _____ □ _____

8. Great peace have they who love your law, and nothing can make them stumble. *Psalm 119:165 (NIV)*
□ _____ □ _____

9. Do not be anxious about anything, but in everything by prayer and petition, with thanksgiving, present your requests to God. And the peace of God, which transcends all understanding, will guard your hearts and your minds in Christ Jesus. *Philippians 4:6, 7 (NIV)* □ _____ □ _____

I'm so impatient. Will God help me to wait for his timing?

1. You need to be patient, in order to do the will of God and receive what he promises. *Hebrews 10:36 (TEV)* □ _____ □ _____

2. We can rejoice . . . when we run into problems and trials for we know that they are good for us—they help us learn to be patient. And patience develops strength of character in us and helps us trust God more each time we use it until finally our hope and faith are strong and steady. *Romans 5:3, 4 (TLB)*
□ _____ □ _____

3. In everything we do we show that we are God's servants, by patiently enduring trouble, hardships, and difficulties. *II Corinthians 6:4 (TEV)*
□ _____ □ _____

4. When the Holy Spirit controls our lives he will produce this kind of fruit in us: love, joy, peace, patience, kindness, goodness, faithfulness, gentleness and self-control. *Galatians 5:22 (TLB)*

☐ _____ ☐ _____

5. Be patient, brothers, until the Lord's coming. Think of a farmer: how patiently he waits for the precious fruit of the ground until it has had the autumn rains and the spring rains. You too have to be patient; do not lose heart. *James 5:7, 8 (JB)*

☐ _____ ☐ _____

6. You are God's man. Run from all these evil things and work instead at what is right and good, learning to trust him and love others, and to be patient and gentle. *I Timothy 6:11 (TLB)*

☐ _____ ☐ _____

7. We do not want any of you to grow slack, but to follow the example of those who through sheer patient faith came to possess the promises. *Hebrews 6:12 (Phillips)* ☐ _____ ☐ _____

8. Learn to put aside your own desires so that you will become patient and godly, gladly letting God have his way with you. *II Peter 1:6 (TLB)*

☐ _____ ☐ _____

9. You understand that your faith is only put to the test to make you patient, but patience too is to have its practical results so that you will become fully developed, complete, with nothing missing. *James 1:3, 4 (JB)* ☐ _____ ☐ _____

10. I waited patiently for the Lord; he turned to me and heard my cry. *Psalm 40:1 (NIV)*

☐ _____ ☐ _____

I always seem to pull away from God and do my own thing. Will he help me to obey him?

1. He is able to keep you from slipping and falling away, and to bring you, sinless and perfect, into his glorious presence with mighty shouts of everlasting joy. *Jude 1:24, 25 (TLB)*
□ _____ □ _____

2. God is always at work in you to make you willing and able to obey his own purpose. *Philippians 2:13 (TEV)* □ _____ □ _____

3. I am sure that God who began the good work within you will keep right on helping you grow in his grace until his task within you is finally finished on that day when Jesus Christ returns. *Philippians 1:6 (TLB)*
□ _____ □ _____

4. I shall put my spirit in you, and make you keep my laws and sincerely respect my observances. *Ezekiel 36:27 (JB)* □ _____ □ _____

5. He guides the humble in what is right and teaches them his way. *Psalm 25:9 (NIV)*
□ _____ □ _____

6. I will heal their waywardness and love them freely, for my anger has turned away from them. *Hosea 14:4 (NIV)* □ _____ □ _____

7. The Lord guides a man in the way he should go and protects those who please him. If they fall, they will not stay down, because the Lord will help them up. *Psalm 37:23, 24 (TEV)* □ _____ □ _____

8. I will give them a new heart and a new mind. I will take away their stubborn heart of stone and will give them an obedient heart. Then they will keep my laws and faithfully obey all my commands. They will be my people and I will be their God. *Ezekiel 11:19, 20 (TEV)*
□ _____ □ _____

I'm worried about money. Will God care for my financial needs?

1. My God will meet all your needs according to his glorious riches in Christ Jesus. *Philippians 4:19 (NIV)*
☐ _____ ☐ _____

2. God is able to provide you with every blessing in abundance, so that you may always have enough of everything and may provide in abundance for every good work. *II Corinthians 9:8 (RSV)*
☐ _____ ☐ _____

3. The blessing of the Lord brings wealth, and he adds no trouble to it. *Proverbs 10:22 (NIV)*
☐ _____ ☐ _____

4. The young lions do lack and suffer hunger; but they who seek the Lord shall not be in want of any good thing. *Psalm 34:10 (NASB)*
☐ _____ ☐ _____

5. In all my years I have never seen the Lord forsake a man who loves him; nor have I seen the children of the godly go hungry. *Psalm 37:25 (TLB)*
☐ _____ ☐ _____

6. The Lord is my shepherd, I shall lack nothing. *Psalm 23:1 (NIV)* ☐ _____ ☐ _____

7. He satisfies the thirsty and fills the hungry with good things. *Psalm 107:9 (NIV)*
☐ _____ ☐ _____

8. He who did not hesitate to spare his own Son but gave him up for us all—can we not trust such a God to give us, with him, everything else that we can need? *Romans 8:32 (Phillips)*
☐ _____ ☐ _____

9. Give me neither poverty nor riches; feed me with the food that is needful for me, lest I be full, and deny thee, and say "Who is the Lord?", or lest I be poor, and steal, and profane the name of my God. *Proverbs 30:8, 9 (RSV)* ☐ _____ ☐ _____

10. Do not save riches for yourselves here on earth, where moths and rust destroy, and robbers break in and steal. Instead, store up riches for yourselves in heaven, where moths and rust cannot destroy, and robbers cannot break in and steal. For your heart will always be where your riches are. *Matthew 6:19-21 (TEV)* □ _____ □ _____

Forbidden things seem so appealing. What should I do when I'm tempted?

1. Every test that you have experienced is the kind that normally comes to people. But God keeps his promise, and he will not allow you to be tested beyond your power to remain firm; at the time you are put to the test he will give you the strength to endure it, and so provide you with a way out. *I Corinthians 10:13 (TEV)* □ _____ □ _____

2. The Lord can rescue you and me from the temptations that surround us. *II Peter 2:9 (TLB)* □ _____ □ _____

3. Don't let the world around you squeeze you into its own mold, but let God re-make you so that your whole attitude of mind is changed. *Romans 12:1 (Phillips)* □ _____ □ _____

4. Since we have a great high priest who has gone into heaven, Jesus the Son of God, let us hold firmly to the faith we profess. For we do not have a high priest who is unable to sympathize with our weaknesses, but we have one who has been tempted in every way, just as we are—yet was without sin. *Hebrews 4:14, 15 (NIV)* □ _____ □ _____

5. Submit yourselves therefore to God. Resist the devil and he will flee from you. Draw near to God and he will draw near to you. *James 4:7, 8 (RSV)* □ _____ □ _____

6. When tempted, no one should say, "God is tempting me." For God cannot be tempted by evil, nor does he tempt anyone. *James 1:13 (NIV)*

☐ _____ ☐ _____

7. Blessed is the man who endures temptation; for when he has been proved, he will receive the crown of life which the Lord has promised to those who love Him. *James 1:12 (NKJB)*

☐ _____ ☐ _____

My physical desires are so strong. Lord, will you help me to control them?

1. No temptation has come your way that is too hard for flesh and blood to bear. But God can be trusted not to allow you to suffer any temptation beyond your powers of endurance. He will see to it that every temptation has its way out, so that it will be possible for you to bear it. *I Corinthians 10:13 (Phillips)*

☐ _____ ☐ _____

2. Flee from sexual immorality. All other sins a man commits are outside his body, but he who sins sexually sins against his own body. Do you not know that your body is a temple of the Holy Spirit, who is in you, whom you have received from God? You are not your own; you were bought with a price. Therefore honor God with your body. *I Corinthians 6:18-20 (NIV)* ☐ _____ ☐ _____

3. Sexual sin is never right; our bodies were not made for that but for the Lord, and the Lord wants to fill our bodies with himself. *I Corinthians 6:13 (TLB)*

☐ _____ ☐ _____

4. Do you not know that your bodies are members of Christ himself? Shall I therefore take the members of Christ and unite them with a prostitute? Never! *I Corinthians 6:15 (NIV)*

☐ _____ ☐ _____

5. Depart, depart, go out from there! Touch no unclean thing! Come out from it and be pure. *Isaiah 52:11 (NIV)* □ _____ □ _____

6. How can a young man keep his way pure? By guarding it according to thy word. With my whole heart I seek thee; let me not wander from thy commandments! *Psalm 119:9, 10 (RSV)*

□ _____ □ _____

7. Truly God is good to the upright, to those who are pure in heart. *Psalm 73:1 (RSV)*

□ _____ □ _____

8. We all once lived in the passions of our flesh . . . like the rest of mankind. But God . . . made us alive together with Christ . . . and raised us up with him. *Ephesians 2:3-5 (RSV)*

□ _____ □ _____

9. Food will not commend us to God. We are no worse off if we do not eat and no better off if we do. *1 Corinthians 8:8 (RSV)*

□ _____ □ _____

10. Do not be anxious about your life, what you shall eat . . . for life is more than food. *Luke 12:22, 23 (RSV)*

□ _____ □ _____

11. Don't carouse with drunkards and gluttons, for they are on their way to poverty. And remember that too much sleep clothes a man with rags. *Proverbs 23:19-21 (TLB)* □ _____ □ _____

12. The desire of the sluggard kills him, for his hands refuse to labor. *Proverbs 21:25 (RSV)*

□ _____ □ _____

13. Lazy people want much but get little, while the diligent are prospering. *Proverbs 13:4 (TLB)*

□ _____ □ _____

14. A little sleep . . . and poverty will come upon you like a robber. *Proverbs 24:33, 34 (RSV)*

□ _____ □ _____

15. Everything in the world—the cravings of sinful

man, the lust of his eyes and the boasting of what he
has and does—comes not from the Father but from
the world. The world and its desires pass away, but the
man who does the will of God lives forever. *I John
2:16, 17 (NIV)* □ _____ □ _____

16. Walk by the Spirit and do not gratify the desires of
the flesh. For the desires of the flesh are against the
Spirit, and the desires of the Spirit are against the flesh
. . . the works of the flesh are plain: immorality, impurity,
licentiousness . . . drunkenness . . . and the like . . .
those who do such things shall not inherit the kingdom of God. *Galatians 5:16, 17, 19, 20, 21 (RSV)*
□ _____ □ _____

Some nights I lie awake and worry. Can God help me sleep?

1. The man who works hard sleeps well. *Ecclesiastes
5:12 (TLB)* □ _____ □ _____

2. When you lie down, you will not be afraid; when
you lie down your sleep will be sweet. *Proverbs 3:24
(NIV)* □ _____ □ _____

3. When I lie down, I go to sleep in peace; you alone,
O Lord, keep me perfectly safe. *Psalm 4:8 (TEV)*
□ _____ □ _____

4. He grants sleep to those he loves. *Psalm 127:2
(NIV)* □ _____ □ _____

5. I lie down and sleep; I wake again, for the Lord
sustains me. *Psalms 3:5 (RSV)*
□ _____ □ _____

6. The Lord gave them rest on every side. *Joshua
21:44 (RSV)* □ _____ □ _____

7. There still exists, therefore, a full and complete rest
for the people of God. *Hebrews 4:9 (Phillips)*
□ _____ □ _____

8. "My Presence will go with you, and I will give you rest." *Exodus 33:14 (NIV)*
□ _____ □ _____

I'm confused about what to believe. How can I know for sure what is truth?

1. Know and believe me and understand that I am He. Before me no god was formed, nor shall there be any after me. *Isaiah 43:10 (RSV)*
□ _____ □ _____

2. God gave the Law through Moses; but grace and truth came through Jesus Christ. *John 1:17 (TEV)*
□ _____ □ _____

3. Jesus replied, "I am the way; I am the truth and I am life; no one comes to the Father except by me." *John 14:6 (NEB)* □ _____ □ _____

4. Jesus said, "If you hold to my teaching, you are really my disciples. Then you will know the truth, and the truth will set you free." *John 8:31, 32 (NIV)*
□ _____ □ _____

5. When the Spirit of truth comes he will lead you to the complete truth, since he will not be speaking as from himself but will say only what he has learned. *John 16:13 (JB)* □ _____ □ _____

6. Make them holy by the truth; for your word is the truth. *John 17:17 (Phillips)*
□ _____ □ _____

7. Behold, Thou dost desire truth in the innermost being, and in the hidden part Thou wilt make me know wisdom. *Psalm 51:6 (NASB)*
□ _____ □ _____

8. Let not your hearts be troubled; believe in God, believe also in me. *John 14:1 (RSV)*
□ _____ □ _____

9. He who saw it has borne witness—his testimony is true, and he knows that he tells the truth—that you also may believe. For these things took place that the scripture might be fulfilled. *John 19:35, 36 (RSV)*
□ _____ □ _____

10. Believe on the Lord Jesus Christ and you will be saved, you and your household. *Acts 16:31 (RSV)*
□ _____ □ _____

11. Jesus said to (Thomas), "Have you believed because you have seen me? Blessed are those who have not seen and yet believe." *John 20:29 (RSV)*
□ _____ □ _____

12. Finally brothers, fill your minds with everything that is true, everything that is noble, everything that is good and pure, everything that we love and honour, and everything that can be thought virtuous or worthy of praise. *Philippians 4:8 (JB)*
□ _____ □ _____

I'm scared of growing old. Who will care for me?

1. I will be your God through all your lifetime, yes, even when your hair is white with age. I made you and I will care for you. *Isaiah 46:4 (TLB)*
□ _____ □ _____

2. He satisfies you with good as long as you live so that your youth is renewed like the eagles. *Psalm 103:5 (RSV)* □ _____ □ _____

3. I will carry you along and be your Savior. *Isaiah 46:4b (TLB)* □ _____ □ _____

4. The righteous will flourish like a palm tree, they will grow like a cedar of Lebanon; they will still bear fruit in old age, they will stay fresh and green. *Psalm 92:12, 14 (NIV)* □ _____ □ _____

5. I give them eternal life and they shall never perish. *John 10:28 (NKJB)* □ _____ □ _____

6. Be anxious for nothing, but in everything by prayer and supplication with thanksgiving let your requests be made known to God. And the peace of God, which surpasses all comprehension, shall guard your hearts and your minds in Christ Jesus. *Philippians 4:6, 7 (NASB)* □ _____ □ _____

7. I, the Lord, have called you in righteousness; I will take hold of your hand. I will keep you. *Isaiah 42:6 (NIV)* □ _____ □ _____

I'm afraid of dying. How do I overcome this fear of death?

1. He . . . shared in their humanity so that by his death he might destroy him who holds the power of death— that is, the devil—and free those who all their lives were held in slavery by their fear of death. *Hebrews 2:14, 15 (NIV)* □ _____ □ _____

2. God loved the world so much that he gave his only Son, that everyone who has faith in him may not die but have eternal life. *John 3:16 (NEB)*
□ _____ □ _____

3. He abolished death, and he has proclaimed life and immortality through the Good News. *II Timothy 1:10 (JB)* □ _____ □ _____

4. Where, O death is your victory? Where, O death is your sting? Thanks be to God! He gives us the victory through our Lord Jesus Christ. *I Corinthians 15:55, 57 (NIV)* □ _____ □ _____

5. I give them eternal life, and they shall never die; and no one can snatch them away from me. *John 10:28 (TEV)* □ _____ □ _____

6. If the Spirit of him who raised Jesus from the dead

is living in you, he who raised Christ from the dead will also give life to your mortal bodies through his Spirit, who lives in you. *Romans 8:11 (NIV)*
□ _____ □ _____

7. Our earthly bodies, the ones we have now that can die, must be transformed into heavenly bodies that cannot perish but will live forever. *I Corinthians 15:53 (TLB)* □ _____ □ _____

8. The world and its desires pass away, but the man who does the will of God lives forever. *I John 2:17 (NIV)* □ _____ □ _____

9. The path of the godly leads to life. So why fear death? *Proverbs 12:28 (TLB)*
□ _____ □ _____

10. Even though I walk through the valley of the shadow of death, I fear no evil, for Thou are with me; Thy rod and Thy staff, they comfort me. *Psalm 23:4 (NASB)* □ _____ □ _____

11. He will swallow up death for ever, and the Lord God will wipe away tears from all faces, and the reproach of his people he will take away from all the earth, for the Lord has spoken. *Isaiah 25:8 (RSV)*
□ _____ □ _____

I often say things I shouldn't. Does God want me to guard my conversation?

1. Thoughtless words can wound as deeply as any sword, but wisely spoken words can heal. *Proverbs 12:18 (TEV)* □ _____ □ _____

2. The tongue of the righteous is choice silver. *Proverbs 10:20 (RSV)*
□ _____ □ _____

3. Kind words bring life, but cruel words crush your spirit. *Proverbs 15:4 (TEV)*
□ _____ □ _____

4. He who guards his mouth and his tongue guards his soul from troubles. *Proverbs 21:23 (NASB)*
☐ _____ ☐ _____

5. Whoever would love life and see good days must keep his tongue from evil and his lips from deceitful speech. *I Peter 3:10 (NIV)*
☐ _____ ☐ _____

6. If anyone can control his tongue, it proves that he has perfect control over himself in every other way. *James 3:2 (TLB)* ☐ _____ ☐ _____

7. The more you talk, the more likely you are to sin. If you are wise, you will keep quiet. *Proverbs 10:19 (TEV)* ☐ _____ ☐ _____

8. The Lord hates . . . a lying tongue. *Proverbs 6:16, 17 (RSV)* ☐ _____ ☐ _____

9. Anyone who says he is a Christian but doesn't control his sharp tongue is just fooling himself, and his religion isn't worth much. *James 1:26 (TLB)*
☐ _____ ☐ _____

10. Don't use bad language. Say only what is good and helpful to those you are talking to, and what will give them a blessing. *Ephesians 4:29 (TLB)*
☐ _____ ☐ _____

11. Dirty stories, foul talk and coarse jokes—these are not for you. Instead, remind each other of God's goodness and be thankful. *Ephesians 5:4 (TLB)*
☐ _____ ☐ _____

12. Set a guard over my mouth, O Lord, keep watch over the door of my lips! *Psalm 141:3 (RSV)*
☐ _____ ☐ _____

I know a Christian should be happy. Will God give me joy?

1. I bring you the most joyful news ever announced, and it is for everyone! The Savior—yes, the Messiah, the Lord—has been born. *Luke 2:10 (TLB)*

☐ _____ ☐ _____

2. God has brought me joy and laughter. Everyone who hears about it will laugh with me. *Genesis 21:6 (TEV)* ☐ _____ ☐ _____

3. I will rejoice in the Lord, I will joy in the God of my salvation. *Habakkuk 3:18 (RSV)*

☐ _____ ☐ _____

4. You will show me the path that leads to life; your presence fills me with joy and brings me pleasure for ever. *Psalm 16: 11 (TEV)*

☐ _____ ☐ _____

5. Praise the Lord! For all who fear God and trust in him are blessed beyond expression. Yes, happy is the man who delights in doing his commands. *Psalm 112:1 (TLB)* ☐ _____ ☐ _____

6. Our mouths were filled with laughter, our tongues with songs of joy. Then it was said among the nations, "The Lord has done great things for them." The Lord has done great things for us, and we are filled with joy. *Psalm 126:2, 3 (NIV)*

☐ _____ ☐ _____

7. All who find safety in you will rejoice; they can always sing for joy. Protect those who love you; because of you they are truly happy. *Psalm 5:11 (TEV)*

☐ _____ ☐ _____

8. I delight greatly in the Lord; my soul rejoices in my God. For he has clothed me with garments of salvation. *Isaiah 61:10 (NIV)*

☐ _____ ☐ _____

9. The Spirit of the Sovereign Lord is on me . . to comfort all who mourn, and provide for those who grieve in Zion—to bestow on them . . . the oil of gladness instead of mourning, and a garment of praise instead of a spirit of despair. *Isaiah 61:1-3 (NIV)*

☐ _____ ☐ _____

Sometimes I wonder why I'm here. Can God motivate me and give my life meaning?

1. Let your roots grow down into him and draw up nourishment from him. See that you go on growing in the Lord, and become strong and vigorous in the truth you were taught. Let your lives overflow with joy and thanksgiving for all he has done. *Colossians 2:7 (TLB)*

☐ _____ ☐ _____

2. May our Lord Jesus Christ himself and God our Father, who loved us and by his grace gave us eternal encouragement and good hope, encourage your hearts and strengthen you in every good deed and word. *II Thessalonians 2:16, 17 (NIV)*

☐ _____ ☐ _____

3. For it is God who is at work within you, giving you the will and the power to achieve his purpose. *Philippians 2:13 (Phillips)*

☐ _____ ☐ _____

4. You will show me the path that leads to life; your presence fills me with joy and brings me pleasure for ever. *Psalm 16:11 (TEV)*

☐ _____ ☐ _____

5. Let us run with endurance the race that is set before us, looking to Jesus, the author and finisher of our faith. *Hebrews 12:1, 2 (NKJB)*

☐ _____ ☐ _____

6. Work hard so God can say to you, "Well done." Be

a good workman, one who does not need to be ashamed when God examines your work. Know what his Word says and means. *II Timothy 2:15 (TLB)*

□_____ □_____

7. We must never get tired of doing good because if we don't give up the struggle we shall get our harvest at the proper time. *Galatians 6:9 (JB)*

□_____ □_____

8. And whatever you do, whether in word or deed, do it all in the name of the Lord Jesus, giving thanks to God the Father through him. *Colossians 3:17 (NIV)*

□_____ □_____

9. As you know him better, he will give you, through his great power, everything you need for living a truly good life: he even shares his own glory and his own goodness with us! *II Peter 1:3 (TLB)*

□_____ □_____

10. Rejoice in the Lord always; again I will say, Rejoice. Let all men know your forbearance. The Lord is at hand. *Philippians 4:4, 5 (RSV)*

□_____ □_____

God's Promises and Purposes for My Relationship with Him

It's hard for me to know someone who lived 2000 years ago. Who is Jesus Christ?

1. Christ was alive when the world began . . . He is God's message of Life. *I John 1:1 (TLB)*

□ _____ □ _____

2. Christ is the visible likeness of the invisible God. He is the firstborn Son, superior to all created things. For through him God created everything in heaven and on earth, the seen and the unseen things, including spiritual powers, lords, rulers, and authorities. God created the whole universe through him and for him. Christ existed before all things, and in union with him all things have their proper place. *Colossians 1:15-17 (TEV)* □ _____ □ _____

3. For God's secret plan, now at last made known, is Christ himself. In him lie hidden all the mighty, untapped treasures of wisdom and knowledge. *Colossians 2:2, 3 (TLB)*

□ _____ □ _____

4. The Son is the radiance of God's glory and the exact representation of his being, sustaining all things by his powerful word. After he had provided purification for sins, he sat down at the right hand of the Majesty in heaven. *Hebrews 1:3 (NIV)*

□ _____ □ _____

5. For God was pleased to have all his fullness dwell in him, and through him to reconcile to himself all things, whether things on earth or things in heaven, by making peace through his blood, shed on the cross. *Colos-*

sians 1:19, 20 (NIV)

☐ _____ ☐ _____

6. I am the way, and the truth, and the life; no one comes to the Father, but by me. *John 14:6 (RSV)*

☐ _____ ☐ _____

7. Anyone who has seen me has seen the Father. *John 14:9 (TLB)* ☐ _____ ☐ _____

8. I am the good shepherd. The good shepherd lays down his life for the sheep. *John 10:11 (NIV)*

☐ _____ ☐ _____

9. So you have everything when you have Christ, and you are filled with God through your union with Christ. He is the highest Ruler, with authority over every other power. *Colossians 2:10 (TLB)*

☐ _____ ☐ _____

10. We despised him and rejected him; he endured suffering and pain. No one would even look at him— we ignored him as if he were nothing. But he endured the suffering that should have been ours, the pain that we should have borne. All the while we thought that his suffering was punishment sent by God. But because of our sins he was wounded, beaten because of the evil we did. We are healed by the punishment he suffered, made whole by the blows he received. *Isaiah 53:3-5 (TEV)* ☐ _____ ☐ _____

Sometimes God seems far away. Will he hear when I pray?

1. I will pray morning, noon and night, pleading aloud with God; and he will hear and answer. *Psalm 55:17 (TLB)* ☐ _____ ☐ _____

2. If my people, who are called by my name, will humble themselves and pray and seek my face and turn from their wicked ways, then will I hear from heaven and will forgive their sin and will heal their land. *II Chronicles 7:14 (NIV)*

☐ _____ ☐ _____

3. You will seek me and find me when you seek me with all your heart. I will be found by you, declares the Lord. *Jeremiah 29:13, 14 (NIV)*

☐ _____ ☐ _____

4. You will call upon me and come and pray to me, and I will hear you. *Jeremiah 29:12 (RSV)*

☐ _____ ☐ _____

5. Before they call I will answer, while they are still speaking I will hear. *Isaiah 65:24 (NIV)*

☐ _____ ☐ _____

6. The righteous call to the Lord, and he listens; he rescues them from all their troubles. *Psalm 34:17 (TEV)* ☐ _____ ☐ _____

7. Ask, and it will be give to you; seek and you will find; knock and the door will be opened to you. *Matthew 7:7 (NIV)*

☐ _____ ☐ _____

8. We receive from him whatever we ask, because we obey his commands and do what pleases him. *I John 3:22 (TEV)* ☐ _____ ☐ _____

9. The Holy Spirit helps us with our daily problems and in our praying. For we don't even know what we should pray for, nor how to pray as we should; but the Holy Spirit prays for us with such feeling that it cannot be expressed in words. And the Father who knows all hearts knows, of course, what the Spirit is saying as he pleads for us in harmony with God's own will. *Romans 8:26, 27 (TLB)* ☐ _____ ☐ _____

10. This is the assurance we have in approaching God, that if we ask anything according to his will, he hears us. And if we know that he hears us—whatever we ask —we know that we have what we asked of him. *I John 5:14, 15 (NIV)* ☐ _____ ☐ _____

Everywhere I look I see evil. How can God be good?

1. Good and upright is the Lord. *Psalm 25:8 (NASB)*
□ _____ □ _____

2. God is good, and he loves goodness; the godly shall see his face. *Psalm 11:7 (TLB)*
□ _____ □ _____

3. Thou, O Lord, art good and forgiving, abounding in steadfast love to all who call on thee. *Psalm 86:5 (RSV)*
□ _____ □ _____

4. The Lord is good and his love endures forever; his faithfulness continues through all generations. Psalm 100:5 (NIV) □ _____ □ _____

5. The Lord said, "I will cause all my goodness to pass in front of you, and I will proclaim my name, the Lord, in your presence." *Exodus 33:19 (NIV)*
□ _____ □ _____

6. Give thanks to the Lord, for he is good; his love endures forever. *Psalm 107:1 (NIV)*
□ _____ □ _____

I want to rely on God and his Word. Will he keep his promises to me?

1. God . . . bound himself with an oath, so that those he promised to help would be perfectly sure and never need to wonder whether he might change his plans. He has given us both his promise and his oath, two things we can completely count on, for it is impossible for God to tell a lie. *Hebrews 6:17, 18 (TLB)*
□ _____ □ _____

2. For no matter how many promises God has made, they are "Yes" in Christ. And so through him the "Amen" is spoken by us to the glory of God.

II Corinthians 1:20 (NIV)

☐＿＿＿＿＿ ☐＿＿＿＿＿

3. Let us hold on firmly to the hope we profess, because we can trust God to keep his promise. *Hebrews 10:23 (TEV)*

☐＿＿＿＿＿ ☐＿＿＿＿＿

4. The God who made both earth and heaven, the seas and everything in them. He is the God who keeps every promise. *Psalm 146:6 (TLB)*

☐＿＿＿＿＿ ☐＿＿＿＿＿

5. Understand, therefore, that the Lord your God is the faithful God who for a thousand generations keeps his promises and constantly loves those who love him and who obey his commands. *Deuteronomy 7:9 (TLB)* ☐＿＿＿＿＿ ☐＿＿＿＿＿

6. For the Lord is faithful to his promises. Blessed are all those who wait for him to help them. *Isaiah 30:18 (TLB)* ☐＿＿＿＿＿ ☐＿＿＿＿＿

7. I will not break my covenant, I will not revoke my given word. *Psalm 89:34 (JB)*

☐＿＿＿＿＿ ☐＿＿＿＿＿

8. I the Lord have spoken; it shall come to pass, I will do it. *Ezekiel 24:14 (RSV)*

☐＿＿＿＿＿ ☐＿＿＿＿＿

9. You have rescued me, O God who keeps his promises. I worship only you. *Psalm 31:6 (TLB)*

☐＿＿＿＿＿ ☐＿＿＿＿＿

I need God's direction in my life. Can I trust him to guide me?

1. If you want to know what God wants you to do, ask him, and he will gladly tell you, for he is always ready to give a bountiful supply of wisdom to all who ask him. *James 1:5 (TLB)* ☐＿＿＿＿＿ ☐＿＿＿＿＿

2. He guides the humble in what is right and teaches them his way. *Psalm 25:9 (NIV)*

☐ _____ ☐ _____

3. Those who obey the Lord will learn from him the path they should follow. *Psalm 25:12 (TEV)*

☐ _____ ☐ _____

4. I will instruct you, and teach you the way to go; I will watch over you and be your adviser. *Psalm 32:8 (JB)*

☐ _____ ☐ _____

5. Whether you turn to the right or to the left, your ears will hear a Voice behind you, saying, "This is the way; walk in it." *Isaiah 30:21 (NIV)*

☐ _____ ☐ _____

6. The Lord will guide you continually, and satisfy your desire with good things. *Isaiah 58:11 (RSV)*

☐ _____ ☐ _____

7. He will never let me stumble, slip or fall. For he is always watching, never sleeping. *Psalm 121:3, 4 (TLB)*

☐ _____ ☐ _____

8. You may make your plans, but God directs your actions. *Proverbs 16:9 (TEV)*

☐ _____ ☐ _____

9. Your word is a lamp to guide me and a light for my path. *Psalm 119:105 (TEV)*

☐ _____ ☐ _____

10. You will keep on guiding me all my life with your wisdom and counsel; and afterwards receive me into the glories of heaven! *Psalm 73:24 (TLB)*

☐ _____ ☐ _____

I try to obey God. Will he respond to my obedience?

1. If you will obey me and keep my covenant, you will be my own people. The whole earth is mine, but you will be my chosen people. *Exodus 19:5 (TEV)*

☐ _____ ☐ _____

2. You shall keep his statutes and his commandments, which I command you this day, that it may go well with you, and with your children after you, and that you may prolong your days in the land which the Lord your God gives you for ever. *Deuteronomy 4:40 (RSV)* ☐ _____ ☐ _____

3. The Lord your God is the faithful God who for a thousand generations keeps his promises and constantly loves those who love him and who obey his commands. *Deuteronomy 7:9 (TLB)*

☐ _____ ☐ _____

4. I will honor those who honor me. *I Samuel 2:30 (TEV)* ☐ _____ ☐ _____

5. Does the Lord delight in burnt offerings and sacrifices as much as in obeying the voice of the Lord? To obey is better than sacrifice, and to heed is better than the fat of rams. *I Samuel 15:22 (NIV)*

☐ _____ ☐ _____

6. All who fear God and trust in him are blessed beyond expression. Yes, happy is the man who delights in doing his commands. *Psalm 112:1 (TLB)*

☐ _____ ☐ _____

7. Obey my voice, and I will be your God, and you will be My people; and you will walk in all the way which I command you, that it may be well with you. *Jeremiah 7:23 (NASB)* ☐ _____ ☐ _____

8. I beg you to obey the Lord's message; then all will go well with you. *Jeremiah 38:20 (TEV)*

☐ _____ ☐ _____

9. Jesus became the Giver of eternal salvation to all those who obey him. *Hebrews 5:9 (TLB)*

☐ _____ ☐ _____

10. How happy are those who hear the word of God and obey it. *Luke 11:28 (TEV)*

☐ _____ ☐ _____

Can I trust God to be in control in the world?

1. And Jesus came and said to them, "All authority in heaven and on earth has been given to me." *Matthew 28:18 (RSV)* □ _____ □ _____

2. The Lord is still in his holy temple; he still rules from heaven. He closely watches everything that happens here on earth. *Psalm 11:4 (TLB)*
□ _____ □ _____

3. There is no authority except that which God has established. The authorities that exist have been established by God. *Romans 13:1 (NIV)*
□ _____ □ _____

4. "I am the Lord, the God of all mankind. Is anything too hard for me?" *Jeremiah 32:27 (NIV)*
□ _____ □ _____

5. O Lord God! You have made the heavens and earth by your great power; nothing is too hard for you! *Jeremiah 32:17 (TLB)*
□ _____ □ _____

6. The Lord our God the Almighty reigns! *Revelation 19:6 (RSV)* □ _____ □ _____

7. The heavens are yours, and yours also the earth; you founded the world and all that is in it. *Psalm 89:11 (NIV)* □ _____ □ _____

8. Great is our Lord and mighty in power; his understanding has no limit. *Psalm 147:5 (NIV)*
□ _____ □ _____

9. Power belongs to God. *Psalm 62:11 (RSV)*
□ _____ □ _____

10. I alone am God; no other god is real. I kill and I give life, I wound and I heal, and no one can oppose what I do. *Deuteronomy 32:39 (TEV)*
□ _____ □ _____

11. Yours, O Lord, is the greatness and the power and the glory and the majesty and the splendor, for everything in heaven and earth is yours. Yours, O Lord, is the kingdom; you are exalted as head over all. Wealth and honor come from you; you are the ruler of all things. In your hands are strength and power to exalt and give strength to all. *I Chronicles 29:11, 12 (NIV)* □ _____ □ _____

The power of evil is so strong. Will God protect me from Satan?

1. He has rescued us out of the darkness and gloom of Satan's kingdom and brought us into the kingdom of his dear Son who bought our freedom with his blood and forgave us all our sins. *Colossians 1:13, 14 (TLB)* □ _____ □ _____

2. The Son of God appeared for this very reason, to destroy what the Devil had done. *I John 3:8 (TEV)* □ _____ □ _____

3. Submit yourselves to God. Resist the devil, and he will flee from you. *James 4:7 (NIV)* □ _____ □ _____

4. The Lord is faithful. He will strengthen you and keep you safe from the Evil one. *II Thessalonians 3:3 (TEV)* □ _____ □ _____

5. The God of peace will soon crush Satan under your feet. *Romans 16:20 (NIV)* □ _____ □ _____ .

6. Listen! I have given you authority, so that you can walk on snakes and scorpions, and over all the power of the Enemy, and nothing will hurt you. *Luke 10:19 (TEV)* □ _____ □ _____

7. My sheep hear my Voice, and I know them, and they follow me; and I give them eternal life, and they shall never perish, and no one shall snatch them out of my hand . . . no one is able to snatch them out of the

Father's hand. *John 10:27, 28 (RSV)*

□_____ □_____

8. If you make the Most High your dwelling—even the Lord, who is my refuge—then no harm will befall you, no disaster will come near your tent. *Psalm 91:9, 10 (NIV)* □_____ □_____

9. The Lord will protect you from all danger; he will keep you safe. He will protect you as you come and go now and for ever. *Psalm 121:7, 8 (TEV)*

□_____ □_____

10. For I am offering you my deliverance; not in the distant future, but right now! I am ready to save you. *Isaiah 46:13 (TLB)* □_____ □_____

People have such different views of God. How does he give me true understanding about himself?

1. It is He who reveals the profound and hidden things; He knows what is in the darkness, and the light dwells with him. *Daniel 2:22 (NASB)*

□_____ □_____

2. I will lead the blind by ways they have not known, along unfamiliar paths I will guide them; I will turn the darkness into light before them and make the rough places smooth. These are the things I will do; I will not forsake them. *Isaiah 42:16 (NIV)*

□_____ □_____

3. He led forth his own people like a flock, guiding them safely through the wilderness. *Psalm 78:52 (TLB)* □_____ □_____

4. The unfolding of thy words gives light; it imparts understanding to the simple. *Psalm 119:130 (RSV)*

□_____ □_____

5. He opened their minds so they could understand

the Scriptures. *Luke 24:45 (NIV)*

☐ _____ ☐ _____

6. When the Spirit of truth comes he will lead you to the complete truth. *John 16:13 (JB)*

☐ _____ ☐ _____

7. He has enriched your whole life. He has helped you speak out for him and has given you a full understanding of the truth. *I Corinthians 1:5 (TLB)*

☐ _____ ☐ _____

8. You will keep on guiding me all my life with your wisdom and counsel; and afterwards receive me into the glories of heaven! *Psalm 73:24 (TLB)*

☐ _____ ☐ _____

I need to experience God's power. What difference will he make in my life?

1. If anyone is in Christ, he is a new creation; the old has gone, the new has come! *II Corinthians 5:17 (NIV)*

☐ _____ ☐ _____

2. I tell you the truth, anyone who has faith in me will do what I have been doing. He will do even greater things than these, because I am going to the Father. *John 14:12 (NIV)* ☐ _____ ☐ _____

3. But you will receive power when the Holy Spirit comes on you; and you will be my witnesses. *Acts 1:8 (NIV)* ☐ _____ ☐ _____

4. He gives power to the faint, and to him who has no might he increases strength. *Isaiah 40:29 (RSV)*

☐ _____ ☐ _____

5. If you have faith as small as a mustard seed, you can say to this mountain, "Move from here to there" and it will move. Nothing will be impossible for you. *Matthew 17:20 (NIV)*

☐ _____ ☐ _____

6. If two of you agree on earth about anything they ask, it will be done for them by my Father in heaven. *Matthew 18:19 (RSV)*

☐ _____ ☐ _____

7. Tremendous power is made available through a good man's earnest prayer. Do you remember Elijah? He was a man as human as we are but he prayed earnestly that it should not rain. In fact, not a drop fell on the land for three and a half years. Then he prayed again, the heavens gave the rain and the earth sprouted with vegetation again. *James 5:16-18 (Phillips)*

☐ _____ ☐ _____

8. For he does wonderful miracles, marvels without number. He sends the rain upon the earth to water the fields, and gives prosperity to the poor and humble, and takes sufferers to safety. *Job 5:9, 10 (TLB)*

☐ _____ ☐ _____

9. How tremendous is the power available to us who believe in God. *Ephesians 1:19, 20 (Phillips)*

☐ _____ ☐ _____

10. Now glory be to God who by his mighty power at work within us is able to do far more than we would ever dare to ask or even dream of—infinitely beyond our highest prayers, desires, thoughts, or hopes. *Ephesians 3:20 (TLB)*

☐ _____ ☐ _____

The Holy Spirit sounds so mysterious. Who is he and what does he do?

1. Repent and be baptized, every one of you, in the name of Jesus Christ so that your sins may be forgiven. And you will receive the gift of the Holy Spirit. *Acts 2:38 (NIV)*

☐ _____ ☐ _____

2. The man who does obey God's commands lives in God and God lives in him, and the guarantee of his presence within us is the Spirit he has given us. *I John 3:24 (Phillips)* □ _____ □ _____

3. He has put his brand upon us—his mark of ownership—and given us his Holy Spirit in our hearts as guarantee that we belong to him, and as the first installment of all that he is going to give us. *II Corinthians 1:22 (TLB)*
□ _____ □ _____

4. You too have been stamped with the seal of the Holy Spirit of the Promise, the pledge of our inheritance which brings freedom for those whom God has taken for his own, to make his glory praised. *Ephesians 1:13, 14 (JB)*
□ _____ □ _____

5. Already we have the love of God flooding through our hearts by the Holy Spirit given to us. *Romans 5:5 (Phillips)* □ _____ □ _____

6. The Counselor, the Holy Spirit, whom the Father will send in my name, will teach you all things and will remind you of everything I have said to you. *John 14:26 (NIV)* □ _____ □ _____

7. But it was to us that God made known his secret, by means of his Spirit. The Spirit searches everything, even the hidden depths of God's purposes. *I Corinthians 2:10 (TEV)* □ _____ □ _____

8. The Spirit too comes to help us in our weakness. For when we cannot choose words in order to pray properly, the Spirit himself expresses our plea in a way that could never be put into words. And God who knows everything in our hearts knows perfectly well what he means, and that the pleas of the saints expressed by the Spirit are according to the mind of God. *Romans 8:26, 27 (JB)*
□ _____ □ _____

9. Now the Lord is the Spirit; and where the Spirit of

the Lord is, there is liberty. *II Corinthians 3:17 (NKJB)*

☐ _____ ☐ _____

10. The law of the Spirit, which brings us life in union with Christ Jesus, has set me free from the law of sin and death. *Romans 8:2 (TEV)*

☐ _____ ☐ _____

I know I should read God's Word. Is the Bible relevant for me?

1. The whole Bible was given to us by inspiration from God and is useful to teach us what is true and to make us realize what is wrong in our lives; it straightens us out and helps us do what is right. *II Timothy 3:16 (TLB)* ☐ _____ ☐ _____

2. Your words are what sustain me; they are food to my hungry soul. They bring joy to my sorrowing heart and delight me. *Jeremiah 15:16 (TLB)*

☐ _____ ☐ _____

3. Your word is a lamp to my feet and a light for my path. *Psalm 119:105 (NIV)*

☐ _____ ☐ _____

4. The word of God is living and active. Sharper than any double-edged sword, it penetrates even to dividing soul and spirit, joints and marrow; it judges the thoughts and attitudes of the heart. *Hebrews 4:12 (NIV)* ☐ _____ ☐ _____

5. The unfolding of thy words gives light; it imparts understanding to the simple. *Psalm 119:130 (RSV)*

☐ _____ ☐ _____

6. Man does not live on bread alone, but on every word that comes from the mouth of God. *Matthew 4:4 (NIV)* ☐ _____ ☐ _____

7. Heaven and earth will disappear, but my words remain forever. *Matthew 24:35 (TLB)*

☐ _____ ☐ _____

8. The word that I speak—it will not fail to do what I plan for it; it will do everything I send it to do. *Isaiah 55:11 (TEV)* ☐ _____ ☐ _____

9. Make them holy by the truth; for your word is the truth. *John 17:17 (Phillips)*
☐ _____ ☐ _____

10. This book of the law shall not depart out of your mouth, but you shall meditate on it day and night, that you may be careful to do according to all that is written in it; for then you shall make your way prosperous, and then you shall have good success. *Joshua 1:8 (RSV)* ☐ _____ ☐ _____

God is so great. Am I significant to him?

1. He is always thinking about you and watching everything that concerns you. *I Peter 5:7 (TLB)*
☐ _____ ☐ _____

2. I am poor and needy, yet the Lord is thinking about me right now! *Psalm 40:17 (TLB)*
☐ _____ ☐ _____

3. O Lord my God, many and many a time you have done great miracles for us, and we are ever in your thoughts. *Psalm 40.5 (TLB)*
☐ _____ ☐ _____

4. A man's steps are ordered by the Lord. *Proverbs 20:24 (RSV)* ☐ _____ ☐ _____

5. What is man that you are mindful of him, the son of man that you care for him? You made him a little lower than the angels, you crowned him with glory and honor and put everything under his feet. *Hebrews 2:6, 7 (NIV)* ☐ _____ ☐ _____

6. O Lord, I know it is not within the power of man to map his life and plan his course—so you correct me, Lord. *Jeremiah 10:23 (TLB)*
☐ _____ ☐ _____

7. "I know the plans I have for you," declares the Lord, "plans to prosper you and not to harm you, plans to give you hope and a future." *Jeremiah 29:11 (NIV)* □ _____ □ _____

I don't always feel lovable. Does God really love me?

1. You are precious in my eyes, and honored, and I love you. *Isaiah 43:4 (RSV)*
□ _____ □ _____

2. God so loved the world that he gave his only Son, that whoever believes in him should not perish but have eternal life. *John 3:16 (RSV)*
□ _____ □ _____

3. God has shown us how much he loves us; it was while we were still sinners that Christ died for us! *Romans 5:8 (TEV)* □ _____ □ _____

4. This is what love is; it is not that we have loved God, but that he loved us and sent his Son to be the means by which our sins are forgiven. *I John 4:10 (TEV)* □ _____ □ _____

5. This is how we know what love is: Jesus Christ laid down his life for us. *I John 3:16 (NIV)*
□ _____ □ _____

6. We know how much God loves us because we have felt his love and because we believe him when he tells us that he loves us dearly. God is love and anyone who lives in love is living with God and God is living in him. *I John 4:16 (TLB)*
□ _____ □ _____

7. As the Father has loved me, so have I loved you. Now remain in my love. *John 15:9 (NIV)*
□ _____ □ _____

8. He who has my commandments and keeps them,

he it is who loves me; and he who loves me will be loved by my Father, and I will love him and manifest myself to him. *John 14:21 (RSV)*
☐ _____ ☐ _____

9. The Father himself loves you for loving me and believing that I came from God. *John 16:27 (JB)*
☐ _____ ☐ _____

10. God has poured out his love into our hearts by the Holy Spirit, whom he has given us. *Romans 5:5 (NIV)*
☐ _____ ☐ _____

11. I have loved you with an everlasting love; therefore I have continued my faithfulness to you. *Jeremiah 31:3 (RSV)* ☐ _____ ☐ _____

12. The Lord is merciful and loving, slow to become angry and full of constant love. *Psalm 103:8 (TEV)*
☐ _____ ☐ _____

13. I am convinced that nothing can ever separate us from his love. Death can't, and life can't. The angels won't, and all the powers of hell itself cannot keep God's love away. Our fears for today, our worries about tomorrow, or where we are—high above the sky, or in the deepest ocean—nothing will ever be able to separate us from the love of God demonstrated by our Lord Jesus Christ when he died for us. *Romans 8:38, 39 (TLB)* ☐ _____ ☐ _____

I want to be God's child. Can I truly call him Father?

1. "I will be a Father to you, and you will be my sons and daughters," says the Lord Almighty. *II Corinthians 6:18 (NIV)* ☐ _____ ☐ _____

2. You are my father and my God; you are my protector and savior. *Psalm 89:26 (TEV)*
☐ _____ ☐ _____

3. He is like a father to us, tender and sympathetic to those who reverence him. *Psalm 103:13 (TLB)*

☐_____ ☐_____

4. O Lord, you are our Father. We are the clay, you are the potter; we are all the work of your hand. *Isaiah 64:8 (NIV)* ☐_____ ☐_____

5. For now we are all children of God through faith in Jesus Christ. *Galatians 3:26 (TLB)*

☐_____ ☐_____

6. To all who received him, who believed in his name, he gave power to become children of God. *John 1:12 (RSV)* ☐_____ ☐_____

7. The Father himself loves you because you have loved me and have believed that I came from God. *John 16:27 (NIV)* ☐_____ ☐_____

8. It is because you really are his sons that God has sent the Spirit of his Son into our hearts to cry, "Father, dear Father." *Galatians 4:6 (Phillips)*

☐_____ ☐_____

9. All who follow the leading of God's Spirit are God's own sons. *Romans 8:14 (Phillips)*

☐_____ ☐_____

10. For his Holy Spirit speaks to us deep in our hearts, and tells us that we really are God's children. *Romans 8:16 (TLB)*

☐_____ ☐_____

11. My son, do not make light of the Lord's discipline, and do not lose heart when he rebukes you, because the Lord disciplines those whom he loves, and he punishes everyone he accepts as a son. *Hebrews 12:5, 6 (NIV)* ☐_____ ☐_____

12. How great is the love the Father has lavished on us, that we should be called children of God! And that is what we are ! *I John 3:1 (NIV)*

☐_____ ☐_____

Sometimes I am overcome with guilt. Does God's salvation cover all of my sins?

1. If we confess our sins, he is faithful and just and will forgive us our sins and purify us from all unrighteousness. *I John 1:9 (NIV)*
☐_____ ☐_____

2. In this man, Jesus, there is forgiveness for your sins! Everyone who trusts in him is freed from all guilt and declared righteous. *Acts 13:38, 39 (TLB)*
☐_____ ☐_____

3. I am the God who forgives your sins, and I do this because of who I am. I will not hold your sins against you. *Isaiah 43:25 (TEV)*
☐_____ ☐_____

4. I will purify them from the sins that they have committed against me, and I will forgive their sins and their rebellion. *Jeremiah 33:8 (TEV)*
☐_____ ☐_____

5. I will forgive their wickedness and will remember their sins no more. *Jeremiah 31:34 (NIV)*
☐_____ ☐_____

6. As far as the east is from the west, so far has He removed our transgressions from us. *Psalm 103:12 (NASB)* ☐_____ ☐_____

7. Once again you will have compassion on us. You will tread our sins beneath your feet; you will throw them into the depths of the ocean! *Micah 7:19 (TLB)*
☐_____ ☐_____

8. He saved us—not because we were good enough to be saved, but because of his kindness and pity—by washing away our sins and giving us the new joy of the indwelling Holy Spirit whom he poured out upon us with wonderful fullness—and all because of what Jesus Christ our Savior did. *Titus 3:5, 6 (TLB)*
☐_____ ☐_____

9. Your sins have been forgiven in the name of Jesus our Savior. *I John 2:12 (TLB)*

☐ _____ ☐ _____

10. The blood of Jesus, his Son, purifies us from every sin. *I John 1:7 (NIV)*

☐ _____ ☐ _____

11. He is able to save completely those who come to God through him, because he always lives to intercede for them. *Hebrews 7:25 (NIV)*

☐ _____ ☐ _____

I'm afraid of God's judgment. Will he condemn me?

1. I did not come to judge the world, but to save it. *John 12:47 (NIV)* ☐ _____ ☐ _____

2. The Lord is compassionate and gracious, slow to anger, abounding in love. He will not always accuse, nor will he harbor his anger forever; he does not treat us as our sins deserve or repay us according to our iniquities. *Psalm 103:8-10 (NIV)*

☐ _____ ☐ _____

3. He who hears my word and believes him who sent me, has eternal life; he does not come into judgment, but has passed from death to life. *John 5:24 (RSV)*

☐ _____ ☐ _____

4. Therefore, there is now no condemnation for those who are in Christ Jesus, because through Christ Jesus the law of the Spirit of life set me free from the law of sin and death. *Romans 8:1, 2 (NIV)*

☐ _____ ☐ _____

5. Whoever believes in the Son is not judged; whoever does not believe has already been judged, because he has not believed in God's only Son. *John 3:18 (TEV)* ☐ _____ ☐ _____

6. Who dares accuse us whom God has chosen for his own? Will God? No! He is the one who has forgiven us and given us right standing with himself. Who then will condemn us? Will Christ? *No!* For he is the one who died for us and came back to life again for us and is sitting at the place of highest honor next to God, pleading for us there in heaven. *Romans 8:33, 34 (TLB)* □ _____ □ _____

7. Each believer should confess his sins to God when he is aware of them, while there is time to be forgiven. Judgment will not touch him if he does. *Psalm 32:6 (TLB)* □ _____ □ _____

8. He will keep you steadfast in the faith to the end, so that when his day comes you need fear no condemnation. *I Corinthians 1:8 (Phillips)*
□ _____ □ _____

9. Fear not, for I have redeemed you; I have called you by name; you are mine. *Isaiah 43:1 (NIV)*
□ _____ □ _____

I don't even understand my own needs. Does God know about them and provide for me?

1. Fear the Lord, you his saints, for those who fear him lack nothing. The lions may grow weak and hungry, but those who seek the Lord lack no good thing. *Psalm 34:9, 10 (NIV)*
□ _____ □ _____

2. As you know him better, he will give you, through his great power, everything you need for living a truly good life: he even shares his own glory and his own goodness with us! *II Peter 1:3 (TLB)*
□ _____ □ _____

3. The Lord is my shepherd; I have everything I need.

Psalm 23:1 (TEV) □ _____ □ _____

4. Your Father already knows what you need before you ask him. *Matthew 6:8 (TEV)*
□ _____ □ _____

5. My God will supply every need of yours according to his riches in glory in Christ Jesus. *Philippians 4:19 (RSV)* □ _____ □ _____

6. Don't worry about anything, but in all your prayers ask God for what you need, always asking him with a thankful heart. And God's peace, which is far beyond human understanding, will keep your hearts and minds safe in union with Christ Jesus. *Philippians 4:6, 7 (TEV)* □ _____ □ _____

7. All mankind scratches for its daily bread, but your heavenly Father knows your needs. He will always give you all you need from day to day if you will make the Kingdom of God your primary concern. *Luke 12:30, 31 (TLB)* □ _____ □ _____

8. Take delight in the Lord, and he will give you the desires of your heart. *Psalm 37:4 (RSV)*
□ _____ □ _____

9. I am with you; that is all you need. *II Corinthians 12:9 (TLB)* □ _____ □ _____

Life is full of change. Can I trust God to stay the same?

1. I the Lord do not change. *Malachi 3:6 (NIV)*
□ _____ □ _____

2. For this God is our God for ever and ever; he will be our guide even to the end. *Psalm 48:14 (NIV)*
□ _____ □ _____

3. Thou art the same, and Thy years will not come to an end. *Psalm 102:27 (NASB)*
□ _____ □ _____

4. Before you created the hills or brought the world into being, you were eternally God, and will be God for ever. *Psalm 90:2 (TEV)*

☐ _____ ☐ _____

5. Jesus Christ is the same yesterday and today and for ever. *Hebrews 13:8 (RSV)*

☐ _____ ☐ _____

6. Every good and perfect gift is from above, coming down from the Father of the heavenly lights, who does not change like shifting shadows. *James 1:17 (NIV)*

☐ _____ ☐ _____

I'm struggling in many areas of my life. Will God give me victory?

1. Fear not, for I am with you, be not dismayed, for I am your God; I will strengthen you, I will help you, I will uphold you with my victorious right hand. *Isaiah 41:10 (RSV)* ☐ _____ ☐ _____

2. For the Lord your God has arrived to live among you. He is a mighty Savior. He will give you victory. *Zephaniah 3:17 (TLB)*

☐ _____ ☐ _____

3. You will not have to fight this battle. Just take up your positions and wait; you will see the Lord give you victory. Do not hesitate or be afraid. Go out to battle, and the Lord will be with you! *II Chronicles 20:17 (TEV)* ☐ _____ ☐ _____

4. For everyone born of God has overcome the world. This is the victory that has overcome the world, even our faith. Who is it that overcomes the world? Only he who believes that Jesus is the Son of God. *I John 5:4, 5 (NIV)* ☐ _____ ☐ _____

5. Overwhelming victory is ours through Christ who loved us enough to die for us. *Romans 8:37 (TLB)*

☐ _____ ☐ _____

6. Thanks be to God! He gives us the victory through our Lord Jesus Christ. *I Corinthians 15:57 (NIV)*
☐_____ ☐_____

7. The victory belongs to the Lord. *Proverbs 21:31 (RSV)* ☐_____ ☐_____

8. I will sing to the Lord, because he has won a glorious victory . . . The Lord is my strong defender; he is the one who has saved me. *Exodus 15:1, 2 (TEV)*
☐_____ ☐_____

Discipline hurts. What is the reason for God's correction in my life?

1. God's correction is always right and for our best good, that we may share his holiness. Being punished isn't enjoyable while it is happening—it hurts! But afterwards we can see the result, a quiet growth in grace and character. *Hebrews 12:10, 11 (TLB)*
☐_____ ☐_____

2. Remember that the Lord your God corrects and punishes you just as a father disciplines his children. So then, do as the Lord has commanded you: live according to his laws and fear him. *Deuteronomy 8:5, 6 (TEV)* ☐_____ ☐_____

3. When the Lord corrects you, my son, pay close attention and take it as a warning. The Lord corrects those he loves, as a father corrects a son of whom he is proud. *Proverbs 3:11, 12 (TEV)*
☐_____ ☐_____

4. My son, do not make light of the Lord's discipline, and do not lose heart when he rebukes you, because the Lord disciplines those whom he loves, and he punishes everyone he accepts as a son. *Hebrews 12:5, 6 (NIV)* ☐_____ ☐_____

5. Since we respect our fathers here on earth, though

they punish us, should we not all the more cheerfully submit to God's training so that we can begin really to live? *Hebrews 12:9 (TLB)*

□ _____ □ _____

6. "Turn to me now, while there is time. Give me all your hearts. Come with fasting, weeping, mourning. Let your remorse tear at your hearts and not your garments." Return to the Lord your God, for he is gracious and merciful. He is not easily angered; he is full of kindness, and anxious not to punish you. *Joel 2:12, 13 (TLB)* □ _____ □ _____

7. Come, let us return to the Lord, for he has torn, that he may heal us; he has stricken and he will bind us up. *Hosea 6:1 (RSV)*

□ _____ □ _____

8. Whoever loves discipline loves knowledge, but he who hates correction is stupid. *Proverbs 12:1 (NIV)*

□ _____ □ _____

Sometimes I fall apart under the stresses of life. Will God restore me?

1. Come, let us return to the Lord. He has torn us to pieces, but he will heal us; he has injured us but he will bind up our wounds. After two days he will revive us; on the third day he will restore us, that we may live in his presence. *Hosea 6:1, 2 (NIV)*

□ _____ □ _____

2. On that day you will say, "Praise the Lord! He was angry with me, but now he comforts me." *Isaiah 12:1 (TLB)* □ _____ □ _____

3. As a mother comforts her child, so will I comfort you. *Isaiah 66:13 (NIV)*

□ _____ □ _____

4. His anger lasts a moment; his favor lasts for life!

Weeping may go on all night, but in the morning there is joy. *Psalm 30:5 (TLB)*

□ _____ □ _____

5. If you repent, I will restore you that you may serve me. *Jeremiah 15:19 (NIV)*

□ _____ □ _____

6. I will restore to you the years which the swarming locust has eaten, the hopper, the destroyer, and the cutter, my great army which I sent among you. You shall eat in plenty and be satisfied, and praise the name of the Lord your God, who has dealt wonderously with you. And my people shall never again be put to shame. *Joel 2:25, 26 (RSV)*

□ _____ □ _____

7. What happiness there is for you who are poor, for the Kingdom of God is yours! What happiness there is for you who are now hungry, for you are going to be satisfied! What happiness there is for you who weep, for the time will come when you shall laugh with joy. *Luke 6:20-22 (TLB)*

□ _____ □ _____

8. Dear friends, don't be bewildered or surprised when you go through the fiery trials ahead, for this is no strange, unusual thing that is going to happen to you. Instead, be really glad—because these trials will make you partners with Christ in his suffering, and afterwards you will have the wonderful joy of sharing his glory in that coming day when it will be displayed. *I Peter 4:12, 13 (TLB)*

□ _____ □ _____

I have such deep needs. Is God really enough to satisfy me?

1. I will always guide you and satisfy you with good things. I will keep you strong and well. You will be like a garden that has plenty of water that never runs dry. *Isaiah 58:11 (TEV)* ☐ _____ ☐ _____

2. My purpose is to give life in all its fullness. *John 10:10 (TLB)* ☐ _____ ☐ _____

3. Every good gift and every perfect present comes from heaven; it comes down from God, the Creator of the heavenly lights. *James 1:17 (TEV)*
☐ _____ ☐ _____

4. It is your Father's great pleasure to give you the kingdom. *Luke 12:32 (RSV)*
☐ _____ ☐ _____

5. God will fulfill all your needs, in Christ Jesus, as lavishly as only God can. *Philippians 4:19 (JB)*
☐ _____ ☐ _____

6. Delight yourself in the Lord and he will give you the desires of your heart. *Psalm 37:4 (NIV)*
☐ _____ ☐ _____

7. Because thy steadfast love is better than life, my lips will praise thee. *Psalm 63:3 (RSV)*
☐ _____ ☐ _____

8. "They shall be radiant over the goodness of the Lord . . . their life shall be like a watered garden, and they shall languish no more. Then shall the maidens rejoice in the dance, and the young men and the old shall be merry. I will turn their mourning into joy, I will comfort them, and give them gladness for sorrow. . . . my people shall be satisfied with goodness," says the Lord. *Jeremiah 31:12–14 (RSV)*
☐ _____ ☐ _____

9. The Lord himself is my inheritance, my prize. He is my food and drink, my highest joy! He guards all that is

mine. He sees that I am given pleasant brooks and
meadows as my share! What a wonderful inheritance!
Psalm 16:5, 6 (TLB)
☐ _____ ☐ _____

I feel spiritually dry. Will God fill me with his abundant life?

1. If any man is thirsty, he may come to me and drink!
The man who believes in me, as the scripture said, will
have rivers of living water flowing from his inmost
heart. *John 7:37, 38 (Phillips)*
☐ _____ ☐ _____

2. Springs will burst forth in the wilderness, and
streams in the desert. The parched ground will
become a pool, with springs of water in the thirsty
land. *Isaiah 35:6, 7 (TLB)*
☐ _____ ☐ _____

3. When my people in their need look for water, when
their throats are dry with thirst, then I, the Lord will
answer their prayer; I, the God of Israel, will never
abandon them. I will make rivers flow among barren
hills and springs of water run in the valleys. I will turn
the desert into pools of water and the dry land into
flowing springs. *Isaiah 41:17, 18 (TEV)*
☐ _____ ☐ _____

4. I give water in the wilderness, rivers in the desert,
to give drink to my chosen people, the people whom I
formed for myself that they might declare my praise.
Isaiah 43:20, 21 (RSV)
☐ _____ ☐ _____

5. I will pour water on the thirsty land, and streams on
the dry ground; I will pour out my Spirit on your
offspring and my blessing on your descendants. *Isaiah
44:3 (NIV)* ☐ _____ ☐ _____

6. They did not thirst when he led them through the deserts; he made water flow for them from the rock; he split the rock and water gushed out. *Isaiah 48:21 (NIV)* □ _____ □ _____

7. The Lord will guide you continually, and satisfy your desire with good things, and make your bones strong; and you shall be like a watered garden, like a spring of water, whose waters fail not. *Isaiah 58:11 (RSV)* □ _____ □ _____

8. Rejoice in the Lord your God! For the rains he sends are tokens of forgiveness. Once more the autumn rains will come, as well as those of spring. *Joel 2:23 (TLB)* □ _____ □ _____

9. Let us know, let us press on to know the Lord; his going forth is sure as the dawn; he will come to us as the showers, as the spring rains that water the earth. *Hosea 6:3 (RSV)* □ _____ □ _____

10. Everyone who drinks this water will be thirsty again, but whoever drinks the water I give him will never thirst. Indeed, the water I give him will become in him a spring of water welling up to eternal life. *John 4:13, 14 (NIV)* □ _____ □ _____

I want to worship God, but I'm not sure how. Will he show me how to worship him acceptably?

1. True worshippers will worship the Father in spirit and truth: that is the kind of worshipper the Father wants. God is spirit, and those who worship must worship in spirit and truth. *John 4:23, 24 (JB)* □ _____ □ _____

2. I don't want your sacrifices—I want your love; I don't want your offerings—I want you to know me. *Hosea 6:6 (TLB)* □ _____ □ _____

3. What I want from you is your true thanks; I want your promises fulfilled. I want you to trust me in your times of trouble, so I can rescue you, and you can give me glory. *Psalm 50:14, 15 (TLB)*
□ _____ □ _____

4. The sacrifice acceptable to God is a broken spirit; a broken and contrite heart, O God, thou wilt not despise . *Psalm 51:17 (RSV)*
□ _____ □ _____

5. The kingdom we are given is unshakable; let us therefore give thanks to God, and so worship him as he would be worshipped, with reverence and awe, for our God is a devouring fire. *Hebrews 12:28, 29 (NEB)*
□ _____ □ _____

6. Ascribe to the Lord the glory due his name. Bring an offering and come before him; worship the Lord in the splendor of his holiness. *I Chronicles 16:29 (NIV)*
□ _____ □ _____

7. He has showed you, O man, what is good. And what does the Lord require of you? To act justly and to love mercy and to walk humbly with your God. *Micah 6:8 (NIV)* □ _____ □ _____

8. Who may climb the mountain of the Lord and enter where he lives? Who may stand before the Lord? Only those with pure hands and hearts, who do not practice dishonesty and lying. They will receive God's own goodness as their blessing from him, planted in their lives by God himself, their Savior. These are the ones who are allowed to stand before the Lord and worship the God of Jacob. *Psalm 24:3-5 (TLB)*
□ _____ □ _____

9. With Jesus' help we will continually offer our sacrifice of praise to God by telling others of the glory of his name. Don't forget to do good and share what you have with those in need, for such sacrifices are very pleasing to him. *Hebrews 13:15, 16 (TLB)*
□ _____ □ _____

10. How good it is to give thanks to you, O Lord, to sing in your honor, O Most High God, to proclaim your constant love every morning and your faithfulness every night. *Psalm 92: 1, 2 (TEV)*
□ _____ □ _____

God has given me so much. What response does he want from me?

1. If you love me, you will keep my commandments. *John 14:15 (RSV)* □ _____ □ _____

2. If anyone loves me, he will obey my teaching. My Father will love him, and we will come to him and make our home with him. *John 14:23 (NIV)*
□ _____ □ _____

3. What does the Lord your God ask of you but to fear the Lord your God, to walk in all his ways, to love him, to serve the Lord your God with all your heart and with all your soul, and to observe the Lord's commands and decrees. *Deuteronomy 10:12, 13 (NIV)*
□ _____ □ _____

4. Has the Lord as much pleasure in your burnt offerings and sacrifices as in your obedience? Obedience is far better than sacrifice. He is much more interested in your listening to him than in your offering the fat of rams to him. I Samuel 15:22 (TLB)
□ _____ □ _____

5. What does the Lord require of you but to do justice and to love kindness, and to walk humbly with your God? *Micah 6:8 (RSV)*
□ _____ □ _____

6. Offer yourselves as a living sacrifice to God, dedicated to his service and pleasing to him. This is the true worship that you should offer. *Romans 12:1 (TEV)* □ _____ □ _____

7. This is how we know what love is: Jesus Christ laid down his life for us. And we ought to lay down our lives for our brothers. *I John 3:16 (NIV)*

☐ _____ ☐ _____

8. "Do you really love me? Then take care of my sheep. . . . Are you even my friend? Then feed my little sheep." *John 21:16, 17 (TLB)*

☐ _____ ☐ _____

9. How can I repay the Lord for all his goodness to me? I will lift up the cup of salvation and call on the name of the Lord. I will fulfill my vows to the Lord in the presence of all his people. *Psalm 116:12-14 (NIV)*

☐ _____ ☐ _____

10. Love the Lord your God with all your heart and with all your soul and with all your mind. This is the first and greatest commandment. And the second is like it: Love your neighbor as yourself. *Matthew 22:37, 38 (NIV)* ☐ _____ ☐ _____

God's Promises and Purposes for My Relationships with Others

I am grateful that God has forgiven me. But how does this affect my relationships with others?

1. Be kind to each other, tenderhearted, forgiving one another, just as God has forgiven you because you belong to Christ. *Ephesians 4:32 (TLB)*

☐ _____ ☐ _____

2. Be gentle and ready to forgive; never hold grudges. Remember, the Lord forgave you, so you must forgive others. *Colossians 3:13 (TLB)*

☐ _____ ☐ _____

3. Our Father in heaven . . . forgive us the wrongs we have done, as we forgive the wrongs that others have done us. *Matthew 6:12 (TEV)*

☐ _____ ☐ _____

4. If you are offering your gift at the altar and there remember that your brother has something against you, leave your gift there in front of the altar. First go and be reconciled to your brother; then come and offer your gift. *Matthew 5:23, 24 (NIV)*

☐ _____ ☐ _____

5. When you stand praying, if you have a grievance against anyone, forgive him, so that your Father in heaven may forgive you the wrongs you have done. *Mark 11:25 (NEB)* ☐ _____ ☐ _____

6. If you forgive other people their failures, your Heavenly Father will also forgive you. But if you will not forgive other people, neither will your Father forgive you your failures. *Matthew 6:14, 15 (Phillips)*

☐ _____ ☐ _____

7. If anyone has caused grief . . . the punishment inflicted on him by the majority is sufficient for him. Now instead, you ought to forgive and comfort him, so that he will not be overwhelmed by excessive sorrow. I urge you, therefore, to reaffirm your love for him. *II Corinthians 2:5-8 (NIV)*

☐ _____ ☐ _____

8. My command is this: Love each other as I have loved you. *John 15:12 (NIV)*

☐ _____ ☐ _____

I have trouble being kind to people who don't like me; who hurt me. How should I respond to the hostility of others?

1. Love your enemies, do good to those who hate you, bless those who curse you, pray for those who abuse you. *Luke 6:27, 28 (RSV)*

☐ _____ ☐ _____

2. Don't pay back a bad turn by a bad turn, to anyone. See that your public behavior is above criticism. *Romans 12:17 (Phillips)*

☐ _____ ☐ _____

3. Don't quarrel with anyone. Be at peace with everyone, just as much as possible. *Romans 12:18 (TLB)* ☐ _____ ☐ _____

4. If your enemy is hungry, feed him; if he is thirsty, give him something to drink. *Romans 12:20 (NIV)*

☐ _____ ☐ _____

5. Do not take revenge on someone who wrongs you. If anyone slaps you on the right cheek, let him slap your left cheek too. And if someone takes you to court to sue you for your shirt, let him have your coat as well. *Matthew 5:39, 40 (TEV)*

☐ _____ ☐ _____

6. Love your enemies, do good to them, and lend to them without expecting to get anything back. Then your reward will be great, and you will be sons of the Most High. *Luke 6:35 (NIV)*

☐ _____ ☐ _____

7. Dear friends, never avenge yourselves. Leave that to God, for he has said that he will repay those who deserve it. *Romans 12:19 (TLB)*

☐ _____ ☐ _____

8. You should be clothed in sincere compassion, in kindness and humility, gentleness and patience. Bear with one another; forgive each other as soon as a quarrel begins. The Lord has forgiven you; now you must do the same. *Colossians 3:12, 13 (JB)*

☐ _____ ☐ _____

9. You should be like one big happy family, full of sympathy toward each other, loving one another with tender hearts and humble minds. Don't repay evil for evil. Don't snap back at those who say unkind things about you. Instead, pray for God's help for them, for we are to be kind to others, and God will bless us for it. *I Peter 3:8, 9 (TLB)* ☐ _____ ☐ _____

10. Above all, love each other deeply, because love covers over a multitude of sins. *I Peter 4:8 (NIV)*

☐ _____ ☐ _____

11. Don't allow yourself to be overpowered by evil. Take the offensive—overpower evil with good! *Romans 12:21 (Phillips)*

☐ _____ ☐ _____

God is good to everyone. I want to be like him, but how?

1. I want you to share your food with the hungry and bring right into your own homes those who are helpless, poor and destitute. Clothe those who are cold and don't hide from relatives who need your help. If you do these things, God will shed his own glorious light upon you. He will heal you; your godliness will lead you forward and goodness will be a shield before you, and the glory of the Lord will protect you from behind. *Isaiah 58:7, 8 (TLB)*

☐ _____ ☐ _____

2. The Christian who is pure and without fault, from God the Father's point of view, is the one who takes care of orphans and widows, and who remains true to the Lord—not soiled and dirtied by his contacts with the world. *James 1:27 (TLB)*

☐ _____ ☐ _____

3. Stop doing wrong, learn to do right! Seek justice, encourage the oppressed. Defend the cause of the fatherless, plead the case of the widow. *Isaiah 1:17 (NIV)* ☐ _____ ☐ _____

4. Love your enemies, and do good, and lend, expecting nothing in return; and your reward will be great, and you will be sons of the Most High; for he is kind to the ungrateful and the selfish. *Luke 6:35 (RSV)*

☐ _____ ☐ _____

5. Let there be no more bitter resentment or anger, no more shouting or slander, and let there be no bad feeling of any kind among you. Be kind to each other, be compassionate. Be as ready to forgive others as God for Christ's sake has forgiven you. *Ephesians 4:31, 32 (Phillips)* ☐ _____ ☐ _____

6. You should try to become like God, for you are his children and he loves you. Live your lives in love—the same sort of love which Christ gave us and which he perfectly expressed when he gave himself up for us as an offering and a sacrifice well-pleasing to God. *Ephesians 5:1, 2 (Phillips)*

☐ _____ ☐ _____

7. Let us not become weary in doing good, for at the

proper time we will reap a harvest if we do not give up. Therefore, as we have opportunity, let us do good to all people. *Galatians 6:9, 10 (NIV)*

☐ _____ ☐ _____

8. Let us love one another, for love comes from God. Everyone who loves has been born of God and knows God . . . Dear friends, since God so loved us, we also ought to love one another. *I John 4:7, 11 (NIV)*

☐ _____ ☐ _____

9. My command is this: Love each other as I have loved you. Greater love has no one than this, that one lay down his life for his friends. *John 15:12, 13 (NIV)*

☐ _____ ☐ _____

Other people's actions often irritate me. How much tolerance and patience does God expect of me?

1. Be patient with everyone. Make sure that nobody pays back wrong for wrong, but always try to be kind to each other and to everyone else. *I Thessalonians 5:14, 15 (NIV)* ☐ _____ ☐ _____

2. Live lives worthy of your high calling. Accept life with humility and patience, generously making allowances for each other because you love each other. Make it your aim to be at one in the Spirit, and you will be bound together in peace. *Ephesians 4:1-3 (Phillips)*

☐ _____ ☐ _____

3. Have unity of spirit, sympathy, love of the brethren, a tender heart and a humble mind. Do not return evil for evil or reviling for reviling; but on the contrary bless, for to this you have been called, that you may obtain a blessing. *I Peter 3:8, 9 (RSV)*

☐ _____ ☐ _____

4. Love is very patient and kind, never jealous or envious, never boastful or proud, never haughty or selfish or rude. Love does not demand its own way. It is not irritable or touchy. It does not hold grudges and will hardly even notice when others do it wrong. *I Corinthians 13:4, 5 (TLB)*

□ _____ □ _____

5. The Lord's servant must not be quarrelsome but kindly to every one, an apt teacher, forbearing, correcting his opponents with gentleness. God may perhaps grant that they will repent and come to know the truth. *II Timothy 2:24, 25 (RSV)*

□ _____ □ _____

6. All of you serve each other with humble spirits, for God gives special blessings to those who are humble, but sets himself against those who are proud. If you will humble yourselves under the mighty hand of God, in his good time he will lift you up. *I Peter 5:5, 6 (TLB)*

□ _____ □ _____

7. Put on then, as God's chosen ones, holy and beloved, compassion, kindness, lowliness, meekness, and patience, forbearing one another and, if one has a complaint against another, forgiving each other; as the Lord has forgiven you, so you also must forgive. *Colossians 3:12, 13 (RSV)*

□ _____ □ _____

8. Of course, you get no credit for being patient if you are beaten for doing wrong; but if you do right and suffer for it, and are patient beneath the blows, God is well pleased. *I Peter 2:20 (TLB)*

□ _____ □ _____

9. When the Holy Spirit controls our lives he will produce this kind of fruit in us: love, joy, peace, patience, kindness, goodness, faithfulness, gentleness and self-control. *Galatians 5:22, 23 (TLB)*

□ _____ □ _____

I know God wants me to be generous. If I give freely how can I be sure I won't be left destitute myself?

1. If you give, you will get! Your gift will return to you in full and overflowing measure, pressed down, shaken together to make room for more, and running over. Whatever measure you use to give—large or small— will be used to measure what is given back to you. *Luke 6:38 (TLB)* ☐ _____ ☐ _____

2. You will be made rich in every way so that you can be generous on every occasion and through us your generosity will result in thanksgiving to God. *II Corinthians 9:11 (NIV)*
☐ _____ ☐ _____

3. The godly man gives generously to the poor. His good deeds will be an honor to him forever. *II Corinthians 9:9 (TLB)*
☐ _____ ☐ _____

4. Thin sowing means thin reaping; the more you sow, the more you reap. Each one should give what he has decided in his own mind, not grudgingly or because he is made to, for God loves a cheerful giver. And there is no limit to the blessings which God can send you—he will make sure that you will always have all you need for yourselves in every possible circumstance, and still have something to spare for all sorts of good works. *II Corinthians 9:6-8 (JB)*
☐ _____ ☐ _____

5. Bring the whole tithe into the storehouse, that there may be food in my house. Test me in this, says the Lord Almighty, and see if I will not throw open the floodgates of heaven and pour out so much blessing that you will not have room enough for it. *Malachi 3:10 (NIV)* ☐ _____ ☐ _____

6. Be generous, and you will be prosperous. Help

others, and you will be helped. *Proverbs 11:25 (TEV)*
□ _____ □ _____

7. He who is kind to the poor lends to the Lord, and he will reward him for what he has done. *Proverbs 19:17 (NIV)* □ _____ □ _____

8. Honor the Lord by giving him the first part of all your income, and he will fill your barns with wheat and barley and overflow your wine vats with the finest wines. *Proverbs 3:9, 10 (TLB)*
□ _____ □ _____

9. Cast your bread upon the waters, for after many days you will find it again. *Ecclesiastes 11:1 (NIV)*
□ _____ □ _____

10. If anyone gives a cup of cold water to one of these little ones because he is my disciple, I tell you the truth, he will certainly not lose his reward. *Matthew 10:42 (NIV)* □ _____ □ _____

11. Give to him freely and unselfishly, and the Lord will bless you in everything you do. *Deuteronomy 15:10 (TEV)* □ _____ □ _____

So often, other people have what I want. How can I deal with my jealousy?

1. You are still only baby Christians, controlled by your own desires, not God's. When you are jealous of one another and divide up into quarreling groups, doesn't that prove you are still babies, wanting your own way? In fact, you are acting like people who don't belong to the Lord at all. *I Corinthians 3:3 (TLB)*
□ _____ □ _____

2. Since we live by the Spirit, let us keep in step with the Spirit. Let us not become conceited, provoking and envying each other. *Galatians 5:25, 26 (NIV)*
□ _____ □ _____

3. Love is very patient and kind, never jealous or envious, never boastful or proud. *I Corinthians 13:4 (TLB)* □ _____ □ _____

4. Never envy the wicked! Soon they fade away like grass and disappear. Trust in the Lord instead. Be kind and good to others; then you will live safely here in the land and prosper, feeding in safety. *Psalm 37:1-3 (TLB)* □ _____ □ _____

5. You must not be envious of your neighbor's house, or want to sleep with his wife, or want to own his slaves, oxen, donkeys, or anything else he has. *Exodus 20:17 (TLB)*

□ _____ □ _____

6. Where there is jealousy and selfishness, there is also disorder and every kind of evil. *James 3:16 (TEV)*

□ _____ □ _____

7. Get rid of your feelings of hatred. Don't just pretend to be good! Be done with dishonesty and jealousy and talking about others behind their backs. *I Peter 2:1 (TLB)* □ _____ □ _____

8. A relaxed attitude lengthens a man's life; jealousy rots it away. *Proverbs 14:30 (TLB)*

□ _____ □ _____

I really want to love other people. Will God show me how to love?

1. A new commandment I give you: Love one another. As I have loved you, so you must love one another. All men will know that you are my disciples if you love one another. *John 13:34, 35 (NIV)*

□ _____ □ _____

2. I love you just as the Father loves me; remain in my love. If you obey my commands, you will remain in my love, just as I have obeyed my Father's commands and remain in his love. *John 15:9, 10 (TEV)*

☐ _____ ☐ _____

3. Don't just pretend that you love others; really love them. Hate what is wrong. Stand on the side of the good. Love each other with brotherly affection and take delight in honoring each other. *Romans 12:9, 10 (TLB)* ☐ _____ ☐ _____

4. This has taught us love—that he gave up his life for us; and we too, ought to give up our lives for our brothers. *I John 3:16 (JB)*

☐ _____ ☐ _____

5. Above everything else, be truly loving, for love binds all the virtues together in perfection. *Colossians 3:14 (Phillips)* ☐ _____ ☐ _____

6. If we are living in the light of God's presence, just as Christ does, then we have wonderful fellowship and joy with each other, and the blood of Jesus his Son cleanses us from every sin. *I John 1:7 (TLB)*

☐ _____ ☐ _____

7. If we love one another, God lives in union with us and his love is made perfect in us. *I John 4:12 (TEV)*

☐ _____ ☐ _____

8. All is well, for we know how dearly God loves us, and we feel this warm love everywhere within us because God has given us the Holy Spirit to fill our hearts with his love. *Romans 5:5 (TLB)*

☐ _____ ☐ _____

9. Knowledge puffs up, but love builds up. *I Corinthians 8:1 (NIV)* ☐ _____ ☐ _____

My parents don't always understand me. How should I respond to them?

1. Children, obey your parents; this is the right thing to do because God has placed them in authority over you. Honor your father and mother. This is the first of God's Ten Commandments that ends with a promise. And this is the promise: that if you honor your father and mother, yours will be a long life, full of blessing. *Ephesians 6:1-3 (TLB)*
☐ _____ ☐ _____

2. Children, obey your parents in everything, for this pleases the Lord. *Colossians 3:20 (NIV)*
☐ _____ ☐ _____

3. Honor your father and your mother, that your days may be long in the land which the Lord your God gives you. *Exodus 20:12 (RSV)*
☐ _____ ☐ _____

4. A wise son brings joy to his father, but a foolish son grief to his mother. *Proverbs 10:1 (NIV)*
☐ _____ ☐ _____

5. If anyone does not provide for his relatives, and especially for his immediate family, he has denied the faith and is worse than an unbeliever. *I Timothy 5:8 (NIV)* ☐ _____ ☐ _____

6. Listen to your father, who gave you life, and do not despise your mother when she is old. *Proverbs 23:22 (NIV)* ☐ _____ ☐ _____

7. Pay attention to what your father and mother tell you, my son. Their teaching will improve your character. *Proverbs 1:8 (TEV)*
☐ _____ ☐ _____

8. Respect your father and your mother, as I, the Lord your God, command you, so that all may go well with you and so that you may live a long time in the land that I am giving you. *Deuteronomy 5:16 (TEV)*
☐ _____ ☐ _____

I always seem to argue with my brothers and sisters. Will God help to form better relationships with them?

1. Help your brother and he will protect you like a strong city wall, but if you quarrel with him, he will close his doors to you. *Proverbs 18:19 (TEV)*
☐ _____ ☐ _____

2. A true friend is always loyal and a brother is born to help in time of need. *Proverbs 17:17 (TLB)*
☐ _____ ☐ _____

3. If your brother sins against you, go to him and show him his fault. But do it privately, just between yourselves. If he listens to you, you have won your brother back. *Matthew 18:15 (TEV)*
☐ _____ ☐ _____

4. Anyone who claims to be in the light but hates his brother is still in the dark. But anyone who loves his brother is living in the light and need not be afraid of stumbling; unlike the man who hates his brother and is in the darkness, not knowing where he is going, because it is too dark to see. *I John 2:9-11 (JB)*
☐ _____ ☐ _____

5. If anyone says, "I love God," yet hates his brother, he is a liar. For anyone who does not love his brother, whom he has seen, cannot love God, whom he has not seen. And he has given us this command: Whoever loves God must also love his brother. *I John 4:20, 21 (NIV)* ☐ _____ ☐ _____

6. Let each of you look not only to his own interests, but also to the interests of others. *Philippians 2:4 (RSV)* ☐ _____ ☐ _____

7. You are the people of God; he loved you and chose you for his own. So then, you must put on compassion, kindness, humility, gentleness and patience. Be tolerant with one another. You must forgive one another just as the Lord has forgiven you. And to all these

qualities add love, which binds all things together in perfect unity. *Colossians 3:12-14 (TEV)*
□ _____ □ _____

8. Finally, brothers, whatever is true, whatever is noble, whatever is right, whatever is pure, whatever is lovely, whatever is admirable—if anything is excellent or praiseworthy—think about such things. *Philippians 4:8 (NIV)* □ _____ □ _____

Sometimes my grandparents and other older people seem old-fashioned and rigid. How does God expect me to treat them?

1. Never speak sharply to an older man, but plead with him respectfully just as though he were your own father. Talk to the younger men as you would to much loved brothers. Treat the older women as mothers, and the girls as your sisters, thinking only pure thoughts about them. *I Timothy 5:1, 2 (TLB)*
□ _____ □ _____

2. Give proper recognition to widows who are really in need. But if a widow has children or grandchildren, these should learn first of all to put their religion into practice by caring for their own family and so repaying their parents and grandparents, for this is pleasing to God. *I Timothy 5:3, 4 (NIV)*
□ _____ □ _____

3. But if anyone does not take care of his relatives, especially the members of his own family, he has denied the faith and is worse than an unbeliever. *I Timothy 5:8 (TEV)*
□ _____ □ _____

4. You shall give due honor and respect to the elderly,

in the fear of God. *Leviticus 19:32 (TLB)*

☐ _____ ☐ _____

5. Let the elders who rule well be considered worthy of double honor. *I Timothy 5:17 (RSV)*

☐ _____ ☐ _____

6. Obey those over you, and give honor and respect to all those to whom it is due. *Romans 13:7 (TLB)*

☐ _____ ☐ _____

Marriage is the most important relationship I can have with a person. What are God's conditions for a happy marriage?

1. In the beginning the Creator made people male and female. And God said, "For this reason a man will leave his father and mother and unite with his wife, and the two will become one." So they are no longer two, but one. Man must not separate, then, what God has joined together. *Matthew 19:4-6 (TEV)*

☐ _____ ☐ _____

2. Marriage should be honored by all, and husbands and wives must be faithful to each other. God will judge those who are immoral and those who commit adultery. *Hebrews 13:4 (TEV)*

☐ _____ ☐ _____

3. To the married I give this command (not I, but the Lord): A wife must not separate from her husband. But if she does, she must remain unmarried or else be reconciled to her husband. And a husband must not divorce his wife. *I Corinthians 7:10, 11 (NIV)*

☐ _____ ☐ _____

4. Wives, fit in with your husbands' plans; for then if they refuse to listen when you talk to them about the

Lord, they will be won by your respectful, pure behavior. Your godly lives will speak to them better than any words. *I Peter 3:1, 2 (TLB)*
☐ _____ ☐ _____

5. A man must love his wife as a part of himself; and the wife must see to it that she deeply respects her husband—obeying, praising and honoring him. *Ephesians 5:33 (TLB)* ☐ _____ ☐ _____

6. Wives, adapt yourselves to your husbands; that is your Christian duty. Husbands, give your wives much love; never treat them harshly. *Colossians 3:18, 19 (Phillips)* ☐ _____ ☐ _____

7. The unbelieving husband has been sanctified through his wife, and the unbelieving wife has been sanctified through her believing husband. *I Corinthians 7:14 (NIV)* ☐ _____ ☐ _____

8. Your wife shall be contented in your home. And look at all those children! There they sit around the dinner table as vigorous and healthy as young olive trees. That is God's reward to those who reverence and trust him. *Psalm 128:3, 4 (TLB)*
☐ _____ ☐ _____

9. Be faithful to your own wife and give your love to her alone. So be happy with your wife and find your joy with the girl you married. *Proverbs 5:15, 18 (TLV)*
☐ _____ ☐ _____

10. A good wife is her husband's pride and joy; but a wife who brings shame on her husband is like a cancer in his bones. *Proverbs 12:4 (TEV)*
☐ _____ ☐ _____

11. Live happily with the woman you love through the fleeting days of life, for the wife God gives you is your best reward down here for all your earthly toil. *Ecclesiastes 9:9 (TLB)*
☐ _____ ☐ _____

I want all my family to know and love God. Will he bless my children?

1. Believe in the Lord Jesus and you will be saved—you and your family. *Acts 16:31 (TEV)*

☐ _____ ☐ _____

2. The lovingkindness of the Lord is from everlasting to everlasting, to those who reverence him; his salvation is to children's children of those who are faithful to his covenant and remember to obey him! *Psalm 103:17, 18 (TLB)*

☐ _____ ☐ _____

3. Blessed is everyone who fears the Lord, who walks in his ways! Your children will be like olive shoots around your table. *Psalm 128:1, 3b (RSV)*

☐ _____ ☐ _____

4. Keep his decrees and commands so that it may go well with you and your children after you and that you may live long in the land the Lord your God gives you for all time. *Deuteronomy 4:40 (NIV)*

☐ _____ ☐ _____

5. He who fears the Lord has a secure fortress, and for his children it will be a refuge. *Proverbs 14:26 (NIV)*

☐ _____ ☐ _____

6. Tell the next generation about the Lord's power and his great deeds and the wonderful things he has done. He instructed our ancestors to teach his laws to their children, so that the next generation might learn them and in turn should tell their children. In this way they also would put their trust in God and not forget what he has done, but always obey his commandments. *Psalm 78:4-7 (TEV)*

☐ _____ ☐ _____

7. The righteous man leads a blameless life; blessed are his children after him. *Proverbs 20:7 (NIV)*

☐ _____ ☐ _____

8. All your sons will be taught by the Lord, and great

will be your children's peace. *Isaiah 54:13 (NIV)*

□ _____ □ _____

9. I will bring your offspring from the east, and gather you from the west. To the north I will say, "Give them up" and to the south, "Do not hold them." Bring back my sons from far away, my daughters from the end of the earth, all those who bear my name, whom I have created for my glory, whom I have formed, whom I have made. *Isaiah 43:5-7 (JB)*

□ _____ □ _____

10. You shall rejoice in all the good things the Lord your God has given to you and your household. *Deuteronomy 26:11 (NIV)*

□ _____ □ _____

Living in God's family isn't always easy. How does he want his children to get along together?

1. How good and pleasant it is when brothers live together in unity! For there the Lord bestows his blessing, even life forevermore. *Psalm 133:1, 3b (NIV)*

□ _____ □ _____

2. Love one another warmly as Christian brothers, and be eager to show respect for one another. *Romans 12:10 (TEV)*

□ _____ □ _____

3. No one should be looking to his own interests, but to the interests of others. *I Corinthians 10:24 (TEV)*

□ _____ □ _____

4. Be full of love for others, following the example of Christ who loved you and gave himself to God as a sacrifice to take away your sins. *Ephesians 5:2 (TLB)*

□ _____ □ _____

5. Share each other's troubles and problems, and so obey our Lord's command. *Galatians 6:2 (TLB)*

☐ _____ ☐ _____

6. The important things for us as Christians is not what we eat or drink but stirring up goodness and peace and joy from the Holy Spirit. If you let Christ be Lord in these affairs, God will be glad and so will others. In this way aim for harmony in the church and try to build each other up. *Romans 14:17-19 (TLB)*

☐ _____ ☐ _____

7. May God who gives patience, steadiness, and encouragement help you to live in complete harmony with each other—each with the attitude of Christ toward the other. And then all of us can praise the Lord together with one voice. *Romans 15:5, 6 (TLB)*

☐ _____ ☐ _____

8. Be humble and gentle. Be patient with each other, making allowance for each other's faults because of your love. Try always to be led along together by the Holy Spirit, and so be at peace with one another. *Ephesians 4:2, 3 (TLB)*

☐ _____ ☐ _____

9. Try to stay out of all quarrels and seek to live a clean and holy life, for one who is not holy will not see the Lord. Look after each other so that not one of you will fail to find God's best blessings. Watch out that no bitterness takes root among you, for as it springs up it causes deep trouble, hurting many in their spiritual lives. *Hebrews 12:14, 15 (TLB)*

☐ _____ ☐ _____

10. Now that I, your Lord and Teacher, have washed your feet, you also should wash one another's feet. *John 13:14 (NIV)* ☐ _____ ☐ _____

11. We should be willing to be both vegetarians and teetotallers or abstain from anything else if by doing otherwise we should impede a brother's progress in the faith. *Romans 14:21 (Phillips)*

☐ _____ ☐ _____

12. We who have strong faith ought to shoulder the burden of the doubts and qualms of the weak and not just go our own sweet way. *Romans 15:1 (Phillips)*
☐ _____ ☐ _____

13. Dear brothers, warn those who are lazy; comfort those who are frightened; take tender care of those who are weak; and be patient with everyone. *I Thessalonians 5:14 (TLB)* ☐ _____ ☐ _____

I feel frustrated with my teachers, my boss and other people in authority over me. How can I accept and appreciate the authorities in my life?

1. Submit yourselves for the Lord's sake to every authority instituted among men: whether to the king, as the supreme authority, or to governors, who are sent by him to punish those who do wrong and to commend those who do right. *I Peter 2:13, 14 (NIV)*
☐ _____ ☐ _____

2. You who are servants should submit to your masters with proper respect—not only to the good and kind, but also to the difficult. *I Peter 2:18 (Phillips)* ☐ _____ ☐ _____

3. Obey your masters in everything; and do it, not only when their eye is on you and to win their favor, but with sincerity of heart and reverence for the Lord. Whatever you do, work at it with all your heart, as working for the Lord, not for men, since you know that you will receive an inheritance from the Lord as a reward. It is the Lord Christ you are serving. *Colossians 3:22-24 (NIV)*
☐ _____ ☐ _____

4. Everyone must submit himself to the governing authorities, for there is no authority except that which

God has established. The authorities that exist have been established by God. Consequently, he who rebels against the authority is rebelling against what God has instituted, and those who do so will bring judgment on themselves. *Romans 13:1, 2 (NIV)*

☐ _____ ☐ _____

5. Show respect for everyone. Love Christians everywhere. Fear God and honor the government. *I Peter 2:17 (TLB)* ☐ _____ ☐ _____

6. Would you like to be unafraid of the man in authority? Then do what is good, and he will praise you. For he is God's servant working for your own good. But if you do evil, be afraid of him, because his power to punish is real. He is God's servant and carries out God's punishment on those who do evil. *Romans 13:3, 4 (TEV)*

☐ _____ ☐ _____

7. It is necessary to submit to the authorities, not only because of possible punishment, but also because of conscience. *Romans 13:5 (NIV)*

☐ _____ ☐ _____

8. Pray much for others; plead for God's mercy upon them; give thanks for all he is going to do for them. Pray in this way for kings and all others who are in authority over us, or are in places of high responsibility, so that we can live in peace and quietness. *I Timothy 2:1, 2 (TLB)*

☐ _____ ☐ _____

9. Remind your people to recognize the power of those who rule and bear authority. They must obey them and be prepared to render whatever good service they can. *Titus 3:1 (Phillips)*

☐ _____ ☐ _____

10. Obey your leaders and submit to their authority. They keep watch over you as men who must give an account. Obey them so that their work will be a joy, not a burden, for that would be of no advantage to

you. *Hebrews 13:17 (NIV)*

☐ _____ ☐ _____

11. You younger men must submit yourselves to the older men. And all of you must put on the apron of humility, to serve one another; for the scripture says, "God resists the proud, but gives grace to the humble." *I Peter 5:5 (TEV)*

☐ _____ ☐ _____

12. Submit yourselves to one another, because of your reverence for Christ. *Ephesians 5:21 (TEV)*

☐ _____ ☐ _____

Loving strangers is hard for me. Does God really want me to open my heart and my home to people I don't know?

1. Cheerfully share your home with those who need a meal or a place to stay for the night. God has given each of you some special abilities; be sure to use them to help each other, passing on to others God's many kinds of blessings. *I Peter 4:9, 10 (TLB)*

☐ _____ ☐ _____

2. It is a loyal thing you do when you render any service to the brethren, especially to strangers. *III John 5 (RSV)* ☐ _____ ☐ _____

3. Whoever accepts anyone I send accepts me; and whoever accepts me accepts the one who sent me. *John 13:20 (NIV)* ☐ _____ ☐ _____

4. When God's children are in need, you be the one to help them out. And get into the habit of inviting guests home for dinner, or if they need lodging, for the night. *Romans 12:13 (TLB)*

☐ _____ ☐ _____

5. Keep on loving each other as brothers. Do not

forget to entertain strangers, for by so doing some people have entertained angels without knowing it. *Hebrews 13:1, 2 (NIV)*

☐ _____ ☐ _____

6. Let no one seek his own good, but the good of his neighbor. *I Corinthians 10:24 (RSV)*

☐ _____ ☐ _____

7. Learn to put aside your own desires so that you will become patient and godly, gladly letting God have his way with you. This will make possible the next step, which is for you to enjoy other people and to like them, and finally you will grow to love them deeply. *II Peter 1:6, 7 (TLB)* ☐ _____ ☐ _____

Often I'm with people who aren't Christians. How should I conduct myself around non-believers?

1. And whatever you do or say, let it be as representative of the Lord Jesus, and come with him into the presence of God the Father to give him your thanks. *Colossians 3:11 (TLB)*

☐ _____ ☐ _____

2. Conduct yourselves wisely toward outsiders, making the most of the time. Let your speech always be gracious, seasoned with salt, so that you may know how you ought to answer everyone. *Colossians 4:5, 6 (RSV)* ☐ _____ ☐ _____

3. Be careful how you behave among your unsaved neighbors; for then, even if they are suspicious of you and talk against you, they will end up praising God for your good works when Christ returns. *I Peter 2:12 (TLB)* ☐ _____ ☐ _____

4. Be ready at all times to answer anyone who asks

you to explain the hope you have in you, but do it with gentleness and respect. Keep your conscience clear, so that when you are insulted, those who speak evil of your good conduct as followers of Christ will be ashamed of what they say. *I Peter 3:15, 16 (TEV)*

☐ _____ ☐ _____

5. It is God's will that by doing good you should silence the ignorant talk of foolish men. Live as free men, but do not use your freedom as a cover-up for evil; live as servants of God. Show proper respect to everyone. *I Peter 2:15-17 (NIV)*

☐ _____ ☐ _____

6. My son, watch your step before the Lord and the king, and don't associate with radicals. For you will go down with them to sudden disaster, and who knows where it all will end? *Proverbs 24:21, 22 (TLB)*

☐ _____ ☐ _____

7. Keep away from angry, short-tempered men, lest you learn to be like them and endanger your soul. *Proverbs 22:24, 25 (TLB)*

☐ _____ ☐ _____

8. Don't be fooled by those who try to excuse these sins, for the terrible wrath of God is upon all those who do them. Don't even associate with such people. For though once our heart was full of darkness, now it is full of light from the Lord, and your behavior should show it! *Ephesians 5:6-8 (TLB)*

☐ _____ ☐ _____

9. Do everything without complaining or arguing, so that you may become blameless and pure, children of God without fault in a crooked and depraved generation, in which you shine like stars in the universe as you hold out the word of life. *Philippians 2:14-16 (NIV)*

☐ _____ ☐ _____

I want to share the Good News with others, but I'm hesitant. Will God help me to witness effectively?

1. Quietly trust yourself to Christ your Lord and if anybody asks you why you believe as you do, be ready to tell him, and do it in a gentle and respectful way. *I Peter 3:15 (TLB)* □ _____ □ _____

2. We cannot stop telling about the wonderful things we saw Jesus do and heard him say. *Acts 4:20 (TLB)* □ _____ □ _____

3. Go, then, to all peoples everywhere and make them my disciples; baptize them in the name of the Father, the Son and the Holy Spirit, and teach them to obey everything I have commanded you. And remember, I will be with you always, to the end of the age! *Matthew 28:19, 20 (TEV)* □ _____ □ _____

4. But when the Holy Spirit has come upon you, you will receive power to testify about me with great effect . . . to the ends of the earth about my death and resurrection. *Acts 1:8 (TLB)* □ _____ □ _____

5. Do not be anxious how you are to speak or what you are to say; for what you are to say will be given to you in that hour; for it is not you who speak, but the Spirit of your Father speaking through you. *Matthew 10:19, 20 (RSV)* □ _____ □ _____

6. Pray also for me, that whenever I open my mouth, words may be given me so that I will fearlessly make known the mystery of the gospel. *Ephesians 6:19 (NIV)* □ _____ □ _____

7. Preach the Word of God urgently at all times, whenever you get the chance, in season and out, when it is convenient and when it is not. Correct and rebuke your people when they need it, encourage them to do right, and all the time be feeding them patiently with

God's Word. *II Timothy 4:2 (TLB)*

☐ _____ ☐ _____

8. Since we know that this new glory will never go away, we can preach with great boldness. *II Corinthians 3:12 (TLB)* ☐ _____ ☐ _____

9. The harvest is plentiful but the workers are few. Ask the Lord of the harvest, therefore, to send out workers into his harvest field. *Matthew 9:37, 38 (NIV)*

☐ _____ ☐ _____

10. So is the word that goes out from my mouth: it will not return to me empty, but will accomplish what I desire and achieve the purpose for which I sent it. *Isaiah 55:11 (NIV)* ☐ _____ ☐ _____

11. He who wins souls is wise. *Proverbs 11:30b (NIV)*

☐ _____ ☐ _____

There are so many poor people in the world. How can I respond to their need?

1. There will always be poor people in the land. Therefore I command you to be openhanded toward your brothers and toward the poor and needy in your land. *Deuteronomy 15:11 (NIV)*

☐ _____ ☐ _____

2. He who despises his neighbor is a sinner, but happy is he who is kind to the poor. *Proverbs 14:21 (RSV)*

☐ _____ ☐ _____

3. He will always make you rich enough to be generous at all times, so that many will thank God for your gifts they receive. *II Corinthians 9:11 (TEV)*

☐ _____ ☐ _____

4. God is able to make it up to you by giving you everything you need and more, so that there will not only be enough for your own needs, but plenty left

over to give joyfully to others. It is as the Scriptures say: "The godly man gives more generously to the poor. His good deeds will be an honor to him forever." *II Corinthians 9:8, 9 (TLB)*
□ _____ □ _____

5. Sell all you have and give the money to the poor—it will become treasure for you in heaven. *Luke 18:22 (TLB)* □ _____ □ _____

6. If there is a poor man among your brothers in any of the towns of the land that the Lord your God is giving you, do not be hardhearted or tightfisted toward your poor brother. Rather be openhanded and freely lend him whatever he needs. *Deuteronomy 15:7, 8 (NIV)* □ _____ □ _____

7. He who is kind to the poor lends to the Lord, and he will reward him for what he has done. *Proverbs 19:17 (NIV)* □ _____ □ _____

8. Happy are those who are concerned for the poor; the Lord will help them when they are in trouble. *Psalm 41:1 (TEV)* □ _____ □ _____

9. If you pour yourself out for the hungry and satisfy the desire of the afflicted, then shall your light rise in the darkness and your gloom be as the noonday. *Isaiah 58:10 (RSV)* □ _____ □ _____

10. Give generously to him and do so without a grudging heart; then because of this the Lord your God will bless you in all your work and in everything you put your hand to. *Deuteronomy 15:10 (NIV)*
□ _____ □ _____

Every nation has corrupt officials and government leaders. Will God protect us from their evil plans?

1. The Lord saves righteous men and protects them

in times of trouble. He helps them and rescues them; he saves them from the wicked because they go to him for protection. *Psalm 37:39, 40 (TEV)*

☐ _____ ☐ _____

2. Israel is my vineyard; I, the Lord, will tend the fruitful vines; everyday I'll water them, and day and night I'll watch to keep all enemies away. *Isaiah 27:3 (TLB)* ☐ _____ ☐ _____

3. Will you permit a corrupt government to rule under your protection—a government permitting wrong to defeat right? The Lord my God is my fortress—the mighty Rock where I can hide. God has made the sins of evil men to boomerang upon them! He will destroy them by their own plans. *Psalm 94:20, 21, 23 (TLB)*

☐ _____ ☐ _____

4. I will rescue you from the power of wicked and violent men. I, the Lord, have spoken. *Jeremiah 15:21 (TEV)* ☐ _____ ☐ _____

5. He will cover you with his feathers, and under his wings you will find refuge. . . . You will not fear the terror of night, nor the arrow that flies by day, nor the pestilence that stalks in the darkness, nor the plague that destroys at midday. *Psalm 91:4-6 (NIV)*

☐ _____ ☐ _____

6. I myself have seen it happen: a proud and evil man, towering like a cedar of Lebanon, but when I looked again, he was gone! I searched but could not find him! *Psalm 37:35, 36 (TLB)*

☐ _____ ☐ _____

7. For God carefully watches the goings on of all mankind; he sees them all. No darkness is thick enough to hide evil men from his eyes. *Job 34:21, 22 (TLB)* ☐ _____ ☐ _____

8. In order to set us free from this present evil age, Christ gave himself for our sins, in obedience to the will of our God and Father. *Galatians 1:4 (TEV)*

☐ _____ ☐ _____

Strife and war and crisis rage all around the world. Is God still in control?

1. Those who trust in the Lord are steady as Mount Zion, unmoved by any circumstance. Just as the mountains surround and protect Jerusalem, so the Lord surrounds and protects his people. *Psalm 125:1, 2 (TLB)* ☐ _____ ☐ _____

2. Do not be afraid or discouraged because of this vast army. For the battle is not yours, but God's. You will not have to fight this battle. Take up your positions; stand firm and see the deliverance the Lord will give you. Do not be afraid; do not be discouraged. *II Chronicles 20:15, 17 (NIV)*
☐ _____ ☐ _____

3. Everyone here will see that the Lord does not need swords or spears to save his people. He is victorious in battle, and he will put all of you in our power. *I Samuel 17:47 (TEV)* ☐ _____ ☐ _____

4. When you go to war against your enemies and see horses and chariots and an army greater than yours, do not be afraid of them, because the Lord your God, who brought you up out of Egypt, will be with you. Do not be faint-hearted or afraid; do not be terrified or give way to panic before them. For the Lord your God is the one who goes with you to fight for you against your enemies to give you victory. *Deuteronomy 20:1, 3 4 (NIV)* ☐ _____ ☐ _____

5. No other nation, no matter how great, has a god who is so near when they need him as the Lord our God is to us. He answers us whenever we call for help. *Deuteronomy 4:7 (TEV)*
☐ _____ ☐ _____

6. The Lord will settle international disputes; all the nations will convert their weapons of war into implements of peace. Then at the last all wars will stop and all military training will end. *Isaiah 2:4 (TLB)*

☐ _____ ☐ _____

7. I am not going to leave you alone in the world—I am coming to you. *John 14:18 (Phillips)*

☐ _____ ☐ _____

Prayer Page

| date | prayer |

_____

_____

_____

_____

| date | prayer |

_____

_____

_____

_____

date   **prayer**

_____

_____

_____

_____

date   **prayer**

_____

_____

_____

_____

date   **prayer**

_____

_____

_____

_____

date   **prayer**

_____

_____

_____

date   **prayer**

_____

_____

_____

date   **prayer**

_____

_____

_____

date   **prayer**

date   **prayer**

date   **prayer**

date   **prayer**

_____

_____

_____

_____

date   **prayer**

_____

_____

_____

_____

date   **prayer**

_____

_____

_____

_____

date   **prayer**

_____

_____

_____

_____

date   **prayer**

_____

_____

_____

_____

date   **prayer**

_____

_____

_____

_____

date   **prayer**

_____

_____

_____

_____

date   **prayer**

_____

_____

_____

_____

date   **prayer**

_____

_____

_____

_____

date   **prayer**

_____

_____

_____

_____

date   **prayer**

_____

_____

_____

_____

date   **prayer**

_____

_____

_____

_____

date　　**prayer**

date　　**prayer**

date　　**prayer**

date   **prayer**

_____

_____

_____

_____

date   **prayer**

_____

_____

_____

_____

date   **prayer**

_____

_____

_____

_____

date   **prayer**

_____

_____

_____

_____

date   **prayer**

_____

_____

_____

_____

date   **prayer**

_____

_____

_____

_____

date   **prayer**

_____

_____

_____

_____

date   **prayer**

_____

_____

_____

_____

date   **prayer**

_____

_____

_____

_____

date   **prayer**

_____

_____

_____

_____

date   **prayer**

_____

_____

_____

_____

date   **prayer**

_____

_____

_____

_____

date   **prayer**

date   **prayer**

date   **prayer**

date   **prayer**

_____

_____

_____

_____

date   **prayer**

_____

_____

_____

_____

date   **prayer**

_____

_____

_____

_____

date   **prayer**

date   **prayer**

date   **prayer**

date   **prayer**

---

date   **prayer**

---

date   **prayer**

---

date   **prayer**

_____

_____

_____

_____

date   **prayer**

_____

_____

_____

_____

date   **prayer**

_____

_____

_____

_____

date   **prayer**

_____

_____

_____

_____

date   **prayer**

_____

_____

_____

_____

date   **prayer**

_____

_____

_____

_____

date   **prayer**

_____

_____

_____

_____

date   **prayer**

_____

_____

_____

_____

date   **prayer**

_____

_____

_____

_____

date   **prayer**

date   **prayer**

date   **prayer**

More Books For Christian Living

CLOSER THAN A BROTHER—David Winter's new paraphrase of Brother Lawrence - *Practicing The Presence of God*. A Carmelite monk learns the secret of living close to God.

HOW TO FIND GOD by David Watson—An ideal book for people looking for answers and ultimate meaning in life.

HOW TO WALK WITH GOD by David Winter—For new Christians. Explains how to chart a life of faith, a walk with God.

HOW TO LISTEN WHEN GOD SPEAKS by Chuck and Winnie Christensen—Practical helps for those who want to spend time with God and His Word each day. A *must* book!

HOW TO WIN THE WAR—Strategies for Spiritual Conflict by David Watson - Biblical strategies for the believer's battle with the world, the flesh and the devil.

MY LIVING COUNSELOR edited by Luci Shaw—A daily devotional with morning and evening readings offering God's counsel for every area of life.

100 DAYS IN THE ARENA by David Winter—Paraphrased readings from Augustine, Clement, Ignatius and other giants of the early church. Fascinating!

Order from your favorite bookstore or write:

**Harold Shaw Publishers
Box 567
Wheaton, IL 60187**